Key Account Management

The Chartered Institute of Marketing/Butterworth-Heinemann Marketing Series is the most comprehensive, widely used and important collection of books in marketing and sales currently available worldwide.

As the CIM's official publisher, Butterworth-Heinemann develops, produces and publishes the complete series in association with the CIM. We aim to provide definitive marketing books for students and practitioners that promote excellence in marketing education and practice.

The series titles are written by CIM senior examiners and leading marketing educators for professionals, students and those studying the CIM's Certificate, Advanced Certificate and Postgraduate Diploma courses. Now firmly established, these titles provide practical study support to CIM and other marketing students and to practitioners at all levels.

The Chartered
Institute of Marketing

Formed in 1911, The Chartered Institute of Marketing is now the largest professional marketing management body in the world with over 60,000 members located worldwide. Its primary objectives are focused on the development of awareness and understanding of marketing throughout UK industry and commerce and in the raising of standards of professionalism in the education, training and practice of this key business discipline.

Books in the series

Below-the-line Promotion, John Wilmshurst

The CIM Handbook of Export Marketing, Chris Noonan

The CIM Handbook of Selling and Sales Strategy, David Jobber

The CIM Handbook of Strategic Marketing, Colin Egan and Michael J. Thomas

CIM Marketing Dictionary (fifth edition), Norman A. Hart

Copywriting, Moi Ali

Creating Powerful Brands (second edition), Leslie de Chernatony and Malcolm McDonald

The Creative Marketer, Simon Majaro

The Customer Service Planner, Martin Christopher

Cybermarketing, Pauline Bickerton, Matthew Bickerton and Upkar Pardesi

The Effective Advertiser, Tom Brannan

Integrated Marketing Communications, Ian Linton and Kevin Morley

Key Account Management, Malcolm McDonald and Beth Rogers

Market-led Strategic Change (second edition), Nigel Piercy

The Marketing Book (third edition), Michael J. Baker

Marketing Logistics, Martin Christopher

Marketing Research for Managers (second edition), Sunny Crouch and Matthew Housden

The Marketing Manual, Michael J. Baker

The Marketing Planner, Malcolm McDonald

Marketing Planning for Services, Malcolm McDonald and Adrian Payne

Marketing Plans (third edition), Malcolm McDonald

Marketing Strategy (second edition), Paul Fifield

Practice of Advertising (fourth edition), Norman A. Hart

Practice of Public Relations (fourth edition), Sam Black

Profitable Product Management, Richard Collier

Relationship Marketing, Martin Christopher, Adrian Payne and David Ballantyne

Relationship Marketing for Competitive Advantage, Adrian Payne, Martin Christopher, Moira Clark and Helen Peck

Retail Marketing Plans, Malcolm McDonald and Christopher Tideman

Royal Mail Guide to Direct Mail for Small Businesses, Brian Thomas

Sales Management, Chris Noonan

Trade Marketing Strategies, Geoffrey Randall

Forthcoming

Relationship Marketing: Strategy and Implementation, Helen Peck, Adrian Payne, Martin Christopher and Moira Clark

Services Marketing, Colin Egan

Key Account Management

Learning from supplier and customer perspectives

Malcolm McDonald and Beth Rogers

Published in association with The Chartered Institute of Marketing

OXFORD   BOSTON   JOHANNESBURG   MELBOURNE   NEW DELHI   SINGAPORE

Butterworth-Heinemann
Linacre House, Jordan Hill, Oxford OX2 8DP
225 Wildwood Avenue, Woburn, MA 01801-2041
A division of Reed Educational and Professional Publishing Ltd

ℛ A member of the Reed Elsevier plc group

First published 1998

British Library Cataloguing in Publication Data
A catalogue record for this book is available from the British Library

ISBN 0 7506 3278 X

Composition by Genesis Typesetting, Rochester, Kent
Printed and bound in Great Britain

Contents

Foreword

The concept of pan-company marketing was first championed by Sir Michael Perry, then Chairman of Unilever and now Chairman of The Marketing Council and a vice-president of the CIM.

Pan-company marketing is based on the idea of an organization that competes effectively for customer preference because it redefines its market with great customer insight, lives and breathes customer commitment from the top down, and puts customer satisfaction ahead of shareholder, employee and supplier interests.

Such companies redefine work processes and systems around customers rather than according to traditional functional silos, they inspire their people to invest even better standards of customer service, and they judge their performance against clear customer satisfaction measures.

Their products and services also happen to be excellent and are normally associated with clear brand values. Little to disagree with there – many of us might want to review our own organizations' performance against such criteria.

But is it really that simple?

Professor Malcolm McDonald and Beth Rogers have researched the development of relationships between suppliers and customers from the transaction-based relationships of 'Pre-KAM' and 'Early KAM' through to 'Synergistic KAM', in which a joint team from both organizations works on areas such as research and development, manufacturing and distribution. The role of the KAM manager is to coordinate the work of the multi-disciplinary task groups from both companies.

How does a major world company like Dupont or ICI really maximize its added value to worldwide customers such as General Motors or Ford? It's not easy, and a pound to a penny, the respective corporate structures don't fit.

The pan-company model acts as a framework, but the real answers, as this excellent book demonstrates, are infinitely more complex. Marketing – creating and keeping customers – is a multi-dimensional task. Two-dimensional models sometimes make it seem easier that it is.

Steve Cuthbert
Director General, The Chartered Institute of Marketing

Preface

'Key accounts are customers in a business-to-business market identified by selling companies as of strategic importance.

'Account Management is an approach adopted by selling companies aimed at building a portfolio of loyal key accounts by offering them, on a continuing basis, a product/service package tailored to their individual needs. To co-ordinate day to day interaction under the umbrella of a long term relationship, selling companies typically form dedicated teams headed up by a Key Account Manager. This special treatment has significant implications for organisation structure, communications and managing expectations.'

Tony Millman (1995)

There have been innumerable mighty tomes written about the importance of customer focus and getting close to customers. There can be no closer focus than 'the segment of one'.

The growing complexity of business-to-business markets, which are in a state of metamorphosis from chains of value to integrated recipes of value, present a great challenge. Add the internationalization of business and the growing sophistication of consumers, and you can see why one of the key messages of our research into key account management is that it does have to be distinguished from its predecessor, key account selling.

In a traditional transactional focus, the selling company is oriented to single sales, focused on product features. The outlook of the company is short term. There is a limited commitment to customer service, discontinuous customer contact, and a belief that quality is the concern of production staff.

Companies who have adopted a key account approach are oriented towards customer retention through continuous customer contact and focus on delivering value to customers over a long timeframe. There is a high commitment to meeting customer expectations, and a belief that quality is the concern of all staff.

Key account strategy, of course, has to fit in with the company's overall marketing strategy. Key accounts will normally be the leading players in segments that have been identified as attractive to the selling company. Key accounts themselves can be distinguished by their relative attractiveness to the selling company, and by the apparent fit of company strengths to the customer requirements. We ask the reader in particular to consider customer profitability, which usually grows as the customer is retained over many years.

Adopting a key account approach has implications on the way the company is organized. Customer focus can be achieved through highly skilled consultative key account managers leading dedicated key account teams.

All the indications are that in business-to-business marketing, key account management is not so much of an option, but a customer expectation. Maintaining the momentum of relationship marketing is a considerable challenge in every selling company.

This book is designed to provide a route through this most difficult of terrains. It is a route map which has emerged from the research that the authors have done into the practice of global key account management with some of the world's leading companies. Although there is still much to learn, we believe readers will find this book representative of the very best of best practice.

Professor Malcolm McDonald
Beth Rogers
Cranfield University School of Management

Acknowledgements

We would like to acknowledge in particular the contribution of our colleague on the original key account management research project, Professor Tony Millman. Special thanks are due to him for his enthusiasm for the topic. His previous work, and that of Kevin Wilson, were invaluable in creating frameworks for understanding the development of supplier/customer relationships. Our thanks also go to the work of other colleagues at Cranfield in the field of relationship marketing.

We are also extremely grateful to colleagues who have been instrumental in the production of this book, notably Lee Smith and Fiona Sparkes.

Before you read this book!

Most readers of this book will have had at least some experience of managing key accounts. Some will have considerable experience, not only of managing key accounts, but also in managing others who have responsibility for key accounts. It should, therefore, be quite easy to answer the following questionnaire without having to spend too much time over it.

Please have a go at completing it before you read this book. Keep a record of each individual score and the total score.

You will be asked to complete the same questionnaire after you have read this book and to compare the individual question and total scores to see to what extent the contents of this research-based book have caused you to reassess the efficacy of your key account processes.

How advanced is your key account practice?

How well do you know your key accounts?

Score out of 10:

Do you:

Know your company's proportion of customer spend? ☐

Know their financial health (ratios, etc.)? ☐

Know their strategic plan? ☐

Know their business process (logistics, purchasing, manufacturing, etc.)? ☐

Know their key customers/segments/products? ☐

Know which of your competitors they use, why and how they rate you? ☐

Know what they value/need from their suppliers? ☐

Allocate attributable (interface) costs to accounts/customer groups? ☐

Know the real profitability of the top ten and bottom ten accounts/ customer groups? ☐

Know how long it takes to make a profit on a major new customer? ☐

Chapter 1

The origins of key account management

Introduction

Key account management is a natural development of customer focus and relationship marketing in business-to-business markets. It offers critical benefits and opportunities for profit enhancement to both sellers and buyers. Key account management is an approach adopted by selling companies aimed at building a portfolio of loyal key accounts by offering them, on a continuing basis, a product/ service package tailored to their individual needs. The challenge is defining that approach and integrating it as a process in complex organizations. Even then, the recipe for success is not complete.

The success of key account management is largely determined by the recipients of the approach. Key accounts are those customers in a business-to-business market identified by selling companies as of strategic importance. The challenge is defining what constitutes strategic importance to the selling company. Success also depends on the strategic importance to the customer of the selling companies and what it supplies. The degree of receptivity demonstrated by the customer to a partnership approach is also influenced by the skills of the supplier in meeting customer needs.

The decision-making unit

The origins of key account management lie in the history of industrial marketing. The first theoretical breakthrough in the analysis of the relationships between selling companies and buying companies was the concept of the decision-making unit (DMU), developed in the 1980s. It was valuable because it forced consideration of the way buying decisions are made within buying organizations. It encouraged managers who had been resistant to 'soft' methodologies to recognize the importance of people in the dynamics of trade. Unfortunately, sales management specialists tended to present the human interactions in selling and negotiation as an adversarial interface between sales and purchasing professionals. The approach of purchasing management specialists was equally flawed by a concentration on adversarial approaches.

Relationship marketing

In the early 1980s, the Industrial Marketing and Purchasing (IMP) Group advocated simultaneous analysis of buyer/seller relationships, an 'interactionist' approach. Their model highlighted the interaction process, participants, environment and atmosphere. Relationships were deemed to represent both a valuable resource and an investment: to increase economic and technological efficiency, to serve as an information channel, and to reduce uncertainty.

Their work was followed by the concept of relationship marketing. It contrasted traditional approaches to sales and marketing, which became known as the transactions focus, with the relationship focus, which seemed more appropriate to the market conditions of the 1990s. The transaction focus concentrated on single sales, product features, tactical campaigns, discontinuous customer contact, limited commitment and a view of customer service and/or quality as the concern of specialist departments. The relationship focus embraced customer retention as a deliberate strategy through continuous customer contact, delivering benefits, a long-term outlook, high commitment, and an expectation that all staff would deliver service and quality. Strategic intent and shared internal values became part of the products/services offered. Meanwhile, marketing was redefined as building and sustaining customer relationships. Analogies were drawn with courtship and marriage, emphasizing that a fundamental element of the new concept was ensuring long-term relationships with customers. A correlation between customer retention and profitability was explored for the first time.

The rise of key account management

Until recently, key account management was often dismissed or downgraded to key account selling and selling to major or national accounts. While sales and marketing strategists are convinced that effective key account management leads to increased sales, better profitability and improved sales productivity, beyond the need for a dedicated sales force, the characteristics and techniques of key account management had not been extensively explored until Cranfield's breakthrough research, published in 1996, which explored the characteristics of key account management from the supplier's point of view, and from the customer's point of view.

In hindsight, we can easily identify the factors in the business environment which have led to the ascendancy of key account management.

These challenges were identified in a research report published by Cranfield and the Chartered Institute of Marketing in 1994, entitled 'The Challenge of Change', Tables 1.1 to 1.5 summarize these challenges.

Table 1.1 The challenge of rapid change

Pace of change	Marketing challenges
Compressed time horizons Shorter product life cycles Transient customer preferences	Ability to exploit markets more rapidly More effective new product development (NPD) Flexibility in approach to markets Accuracy in demand forecasting Ability to optimize price setting

Table 1.2 Refining the process

Process thinking	Marketing challenges

Move to flexible manufacturing and
   control systems
Materials substitution
Developments in microelectronics and
   robotization
Quality focus
	Dealing with micro-segmentation
	Finding ways to shift from single transaction
	   focus to the forging of long-term relationships
	Creating greater customer commitment

Table 1.3 The challenge of the marketplace

Market maturity	Marketing challenges
Over capacity Low margins Lack of growth Stronger competition Trading down Cost cutting	Adding value leading to differentiation New market creation and stimulation

Table 1.4 The customer

Customers' expertise and power	Marketing challenges
More demanding Higher expectations More knowledgeable Concentration of buying power More sophisticated buyer behaviour	Finding ways of getting closer to the customer Managing the complexities of multiple market channels

Table 1.5 The international dimension

Internationalization of business	Marketing challenges

More competitors
Stronger competition
Lower margins
More customer choice
Larger markets
More disparate customer needs
	Restructuring of domestic operations to
	  compete internationally
	Becoming customer-focused in larger and more
	  disparate markets

Of these challenges, three stand out as having particular relevance to key account management. These are:

- **Internationalization**
  The internationalization of business has had many side effects. It has led to a greater interdependency between global customers and suppliers who have the capability to meet their ever more complex needs. These suppliers also realize the extent to which they can grow with their key customer if they constantly meet their challenges.
- **Market maturity**
  Figure 1.1 illustrates the impact on the key elements of business management of market maturity. The final column illustrates clearly the danger of allowing products and services to degenerate into commodities with price availability and costs the only ingredients of success. It is this danger more than any other that is forcing suppliers to pay more attention to key customers as a way of differentiation.

  The fact that most industry-to-industry product/service markets in the developed world are mature has clearly influenced the development of key account management. Suppliers know that they can only grow at the expense of a competitor. So, the obvious first option is to price more of existing customers'

Key characteristics	Unique	Product differentiation	Service differentiation	Commodity
Marketing message	Explain	Competitive	Brand values	Corporate
Sales	Pioneering	Relative benefits, distribution support	Relationship based	Availability based
Distribution	Direct selling	Exclusive distribution	Mass distribution	80:20
Price	Very high	High	Medium	Low (Consumer controlled)
Competitive intensity	None	Few	Many	Fewer, bigger international
Costs	Very high	Medium	Medium/Low	Very low
Profit	Medium/High	High	Medium/High	Medium/Low
Management style	Visionary	Strategic	Operational	Cost management

Time

Figure 1.1 The product/market life cycle and market characteristics (based on teaching material developed by Professor Mike Wilson, Marketing Improvements Group)

business away from the opposition by means of account penetration. Highly professional key account management practice can facilitate that objective.

● **Customer power**
One change above all others, however, that is having the most dramatic impact on the development of key account management, is the new-found power of customers in exercising their choice.

Customer power is not just a cultural change from previous decades, no matter how many books have been written about customer focus and its benefits. It is a consequence of mature markets. Customers know that they can demand more of suppliers, because suppliers know that they have to retain customers, not just to maintain profitability, but to stay in business. The nature of customer power manifests itself in many ways. First of all, there has been considerable concentration of industry over the past few decades, and most recently, on a transnational scale, so big customers are getting even bigger. Bigger does not mean more opportunity for all suppliers. Those who cannot meet the geographical scope and consistent outputs that a global player needs are being rationalized off the list. Customers want bespoke, sophisticated solutions, which means that to win them is very costly and retaining them is critical to achieving long-term profitability.

These factors, internationalization, mature markets and customer power, have encouraged key account management away from a single relationship between salesperson and buyer, and the concept of strategic customers as just the biggest has been replaced by more scientific methods. We see companies starting to build models of account attractiveness, matching their resources to the profit and status potential of any given customer or prospect. We see

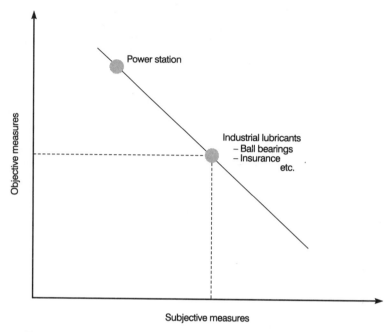

Figure 1.2 Personal relationships and suppliers (based on teaching material developed by Professor Mike Wilson, Marketing Improvements Group)

increasing professionalism in the purchasing profession and decision-making units in buying companies looking at the long-term value being offered by suppliers – product quality, process quality and people quality – rather than at a simple price deal. In the final analysis, however, it has to be people who deliver value to key accounts and even when some organizations have a sound, value-enhancing proposition, they frequently find themselves losing out to suppliers whose people are seen as more caring. Figure 1.2 illustrates that when the offer is about the same from different suppliers, it is the personal side of a relationship that makes the difference.

The purpose of this book

This book is intended to help key account strategists and key account managers to capture and develop a scientific basis for their companies' practice. The scope of key account management is widening and it is becoming more complex. For key account management to be successfully implemented, there is an urgent need to develop reliable diagnostic tools and measures of performance that support strategic marketing decisions. The skills of professionals involved in key account management at strategic and operational levels need to be constantly updated and developed. The book demonstrates how key account management can be implemented and describes the elements of best practice that can be adopted by all types and sizes of organizations.

Chapter 2 describes how the development of key account relationships can be analysed. The model used also provides a useful framework for planning to make progress in relationships.

Chapter 3 puts key account planning in the context of strategic marketing planning. This provides the foundation for Chapter 4.

Chapter 4 explains how to select the most appropriate accounts to target for key account treatment.

Chapter 5 moves on to the kind of data and information necessary for key account planning. It then explains how to set objectives and strategies for each targeted key account.

Chapter 6 discusses the qualities and skills required of a key account manager at the higher relational levels.

Chapter 7 suggests how key account management might be positioned in organizations to achieve the status appropriate to the function.

Chapter 8 speculates about the future of key account management (KAM) as a concept. The underlying trends supporting KAM are likely to take supply chain relationships to new levels of integration.

Chapter 2

The evolution of key account relationships

Introduction

The purpose of this chapter is to examine how key account relationships evolve, and how their potential for evolution can be analysed.

Like all relationships, those between buying and selling companies evolve over time. This process typically exhibits two main features. First, increasing involvement and complexity associated with a shift from 'transactional', one-off exchanges to regular patterns of behaviour that can be characterized as 'collaborative'; and secondly, the building of trust and commitment towards a shared future.

Millman and Wilson (1994) proposed that there are stages of key account management that match transitions on the continuum from transactional relationships to collaborative relationships. This is called the Key Account Relational Development Model. It is possible to assess the position of selling companies at various stages of key account development, analyse managerial behaviour, and gain insights into the changing profile of skills necessary as relationships mature. (A graphical representation of the model is shown in Figure 2.1.)

Relevance of the stages of the relational development model

Key account management is a strategic, long-term activity. From identifying the attractiveness of an account to achieving the full potential of the relationship with that organization could have a ten-year span. Account plans are prepared with the rigour required for marketing plans, using a similar framework, and adopting a minimum 3–5 year outlook (see subsequent chapters).

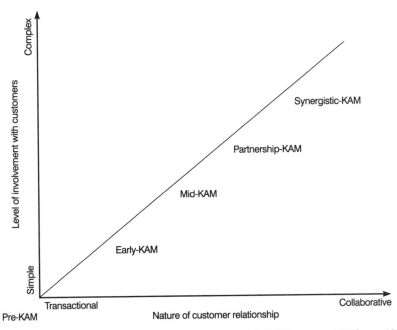

Figure 2.1 Key account relational development model (Millman and Wilson, 1994)

Selling companies practising key account management do consciously plan to move key accounts from prospects towards higher relationship levels. It is clear, that while collaborative relationships are sought, some targeted key accounts are not willing to enter into such relationships and thus remain at the transactional stage. This eventuality, and all variations of seller/buyer relationships, can also be plotted on the relational development model.

This model demonstrates the typical progression of a relationship. In addition to the transactional-collaborative continuum, the progression of the level of involvement with customers from simple interactions to complex interactions is also taken into account. The graph shows five of the six stages identified by Millman and Wilson (1994): Pre-KAM, Early-KAM, Mid-KAM, Partnership-KAM, and Synergistic-KAM. A sixth stage, Uncoupling-KAM, can occur at any time in the relational development process, and is discussed later in this chapter.

The initial positioning of any particular relationship can be plotted onto the model through an analysis of two things. First, consider the proportion of business for a given category of needed products or services that the customer places with the supplier, which can be considered a quick guide to the degree of collaboration between the two. Second, consider the number of interactions between the two companies, together with observation of the number of levels at which they take place.

Pre-KAM

No transactions exist, therefore proportion of business is zero. Nevertheless, the buying company has been targeted, therefore the selling company is trying to establish interaction.

Pre-KAM describes preparation for KAM, or 'prospecting'. A buying company is identified as having key account potential, and the selling company starts to focus resources on winning some business with that prospect. (More information about the identification of prospective key accounts is described later in Chapter 4.) The Pre-KAM stage (Figure 2.2) could be described as a 'scanning and attraction' stage. The selling company is like a spacecraft looking for the point at which to dock in the spacestation (buying company). Both seller and buyer are sending out signals and exchanging messages prior to the decision to engage in transactions. The majority of interactions will be between the key account manager and one main contact in the buying company, who may be a purchasing professional.

The buying company may 'play hard to get'. Many buying companies who have adopted a partnership sourcing approach complain at the lack of suppliers who can meet a long-term challenge. The allegation is often made that the buying company has to teach them! So, at the Pre-KAM stage, the selling company may be quite strenuously tested to prove their worth.

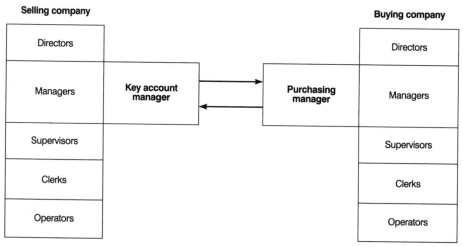

Figure 2.2 The Pre-KAM stage

Buying companies already have *in situ* suppliers, and selling companies should not underestimate the inertia factors that set in. They need to maintain communications while waiting for another supplier to do something wrong, or be sure to be offering a substantial advantage over the prospect's current supplier/s. Even when companies or government sector organizations go out to tender for products or services, the buying company must research the existing solution and find a way in which it can improve upon it.

A British manufacturer of very high technology manufacturing equipment decided to invest in Japan. It was recognized that it was a very long-term project, and the primary activity in the early years was establishing contacts in target companies. After two years, the existing supplier to one prospect failed to repair some critical equipment, and the British company's technicians were invited in to solve the problem. They did, and shortly afterwards that buying company replaced their existing equipment with the British company's instruments, which also offered cost advantages.

A selling company trying to win business with a manufacturer of car parts had impressed the purchasing manager, but they already had three suppliers *in situ*. Then, as part of a quality and traceability initiative, the buying company decided that they wanted a certain raw material delivered on a consignment stock basis. The existing suppliers refused, but the selling company targeting the business agreed. They won 100% of the business and a partnership agreement.

Early-KAM

Transactions have been established, but the supplier is still one of many, so the proportion of business is a small percentage. Interactions are straightforward and mainly at one level, the key account manager/buyer relationship.

The second stage is labelled Early-KAM. The buying company wants recognition that the product and service offering is the prime reason for the relationship – and expects it to work, so the selling company must concentrate on getting it right, enough to convince the buying decision makers that they want more of the same. The buying company will still be using the products of other selling companies. Indeed, some buying companies will always do so, whether driven by their customers' demands for choice, or because of concerns about the risks of 'putting too many eggs in one basket'.

Some buying companies are driven by short-term demands for low prices, particularly in difficult economic circumstances, such as recessions. Even if an account does get stuck in the Early-KAM stage, with buying decision makers unwilling or unable to discuss value and shared best practice, it may still be a key account.

Buying decision makers would argue that some selling companies ground the relationship in the Early-KAM stage due to their organizational tribalism and inability to manage 'hassle', such as sloppy paperwork and poor communications.

Graphically, the Early-KAM stage is depicted as a 'bow-tie', a diagram that emerged from relationship marketing studies (Figure 2.3). It shows the fragility of the relationship, with communications channelled between one main contact from each company. Arguably, if either fell under a bus (or, more usually, if any misunderstanding arose between the two), the selling company's investment in establishing the relationship might be wasted.

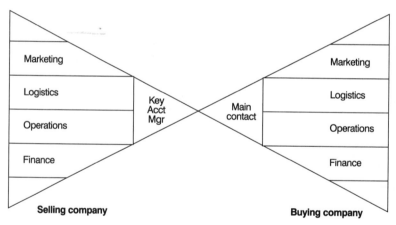

Figure 2.3 The Early-KAM stage

A supplier of technical services to a prestigious manufacturing company was struggling hard to establish its credibility. As far as the purchasing decision maker was concerned, there were two things that jeopardized its credibility. One was dreadful and inaccurate paperwork, and the other was the junior status of the account manager.

A supplier of high tech services to a telephone company thought that it had an excellent relationship with the buying company, although the company was also buying from competitors. The buying decision maker was actually looking for a partnership, and while he favoured that supplier on the basis of its products, he felt that as a company, it just did not listen hard enough and try to make it easier for him to do business. Consequently, he began serious discussions about a partnership agreement with one of its rivals.

'I have to admit, sometimes I push account managers too hard on price. Then everything gets escalated because they can't give us this or that discount and it means hassle for everyone ...' Purchasing manager of the 'adversarial' school.

Mid-KAM

The selling company is now a preferred supplier, so the proportion of business from the buying company may exceed 50 per cent. Interactions have become more complex, and occur between many members of staff in each company.

At the Mid-KAM stage (Figure 2.4), the selling company has established credibility with the buying company, a degree of trust has been established.

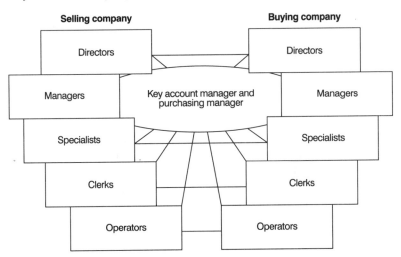

Figure 2.4 The Mid-KAM stage

Contacts between the two organizations increase at all levels and assume greater importance. Nevertheless, buying companies still feel the need for alternative sources of supply. This may be associated with concern about the risks of single sourcing, or a belief in the value of competition. The selling company's offering is still periodically market tested, but is reliably perceived to be good value. The selling company also has the opportunity to provide non-contractual extra services to enhance goodwill. There will be assumed longevity in the seller/buyer relationship, by both parties, even if individual contracts are renewed annually. There may still be clear exit plans as well!

The emphasis switches from product excellence to social integration at the Mid-KAM stage. Everyone in the selling company will be expected to know the names of key accounts and understand their importance to the company, and the service that must be given. The buying company will now know the people in the wider key account team as well, and some senior managers.

It is likely that these contacts will be reinforced by joint social events that involve many levels of staff. Gone are the days of the expense account lunch, companies who aspire to best practice key account management organize skittles evenings or tennis tournaments, which enable larger numbers of staff to participate together, strengthening the thread of the web of transorganizational contacts which is now building up.

At this stage, however, the companies are not necessarily reorganizing anything to suit the other. The main contacts are still papering over the cracks when it comes to process difficulties.

A supplier of chemicals to a food company was considered a preferred supplier, indeed the buying decision maker was very enthusiastic about its competence and 'likeability'. When asked why he did not single source from them, he said that he believed that competition was good for industry, and he felt that occasional purchases from an alternative supplier kept his preferred supplier 'on its toes'.

A supplier of equipment to a services provider enjoyed a product advantage over its nearest rival, but the purchasing decision makers found some difficulties in doing business with them. Their perception was that the account manager took responsibility for their problems, but did not have the power to fix them. So some got fixed in time, but some did not. The account manager was furiously 'papering over the cracks' of the process complexity of the selling company, but until there was significant organizational commitment to 'ease of doing business', the buying company would not give any more commitment to that supplier.

Partnership-KAM

> The proportion of business channelled by the buying company through the selling company is nearly 100 per cent. The complexity of, and the high number of interactions between the two companies have to be monitored via a partnership agreement. Mutual efforts are being made to improve processes to enable both companies to achieve greater quality and to reduce costs.

When Partnership-KAM is reached, the selling company is seen by the buying company organization as a strategic external resource. The two companies will be sharing sensitive information, and engaging in joint problem resolution. Pricing will be long term and stable, perhaps fixed, but it will have been established that each side will allow the other to make a profit!

Selling companies often ask when or if they should go 'open book' with a customer. Only when both companies open their books together is it worth doing, i.e. only when the buying company is prepared to reciprocate should any selling company divulge confidential financial information. Then, it can be assumed that a true spirit of partnership has been achieved.

Key accounts will 'beta test' all the selling company's innovations so that they have first access to, and first benefit from, the latest technology. The buying company will expect to be guaranteed continuity of supply and access to the best material. Expertise will be shared. Both will also expect to gain from mutual continuous process improvement. There may be joint promotions, where appropriate.

The partnership agreement will be long term; at least three or five years. Some partnerships say that, in principle, they put no time limit on their partnership agreements. Several categories of performance are itemized in partnership agreements (perhaps up to forty), and the selling company will be trying for 100 per cent on every measure.

Graphically, the partnership stage is represented as a diamond (sometimes known as the reverse bow-tie diagram). It shows all the departments of each company in full alignment, with the main contacts in the role of co-ordinators. This role is often compared with conducting an orchestra (Figure 2.5).

> 'You can tell that they value us as a supplier. When I went on a visit there recently, all the senior managers of the company greeted me with the enthusiasm they would show to an old friend.' Marketing director of a selling company.

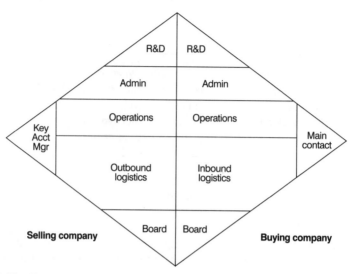

Figure 2.5 The Partnership-KAM stage

'It's the spirit of the thing that matters. Yes, we have partnership agreements and we expect suppliers to perform (and we do our bit), but it is much more than that. There is trust, open communications, we like each other.' Purchasing manager of the 'partnership' school.

In one partnership, when there was an industrial relations dispute in the selling company, both managers and workers co-operated to find a way to minimize the impact on the buying company.

A financial services company that led its market with the concept of key account management included in its partnership agreements the promise to pay compensation if they failed to meet the standards they offer. This was taken as a strong indication of commitment to meet agreements and to act with integrity if something goes wrong. Also, from their key accounts' point of view, they felt that they had been given special status. The decision makers in the buying companies were flattered. They got to know senior managers, they saw the same account manager regularly, and they had access to named people with appropriate technical expertise, and who had been trained to apply that expertise specifically to the customer's industry sector.

Synergistic-KAM

> You can't see the join!

Can there be any greater pinnacle than partnership? Some companies do get even closer. Synergistic-KAM is the ultimate stage in the relational development model. It refers to the selling company and buying company together, creating value in the marketplace, i.e. quasi-integration.

The selling company understands that it still has no automatic right to the customer's business. Nevertheless, exit barriers have been built up. While the buying company is confident that its relationship with the selling company is delivering improved quality and reduced costs, the exit barriers are not likely to be tested. Costing systems become transparent. Joint research and development will take place. There will be interfaces at every level and function between the organizations. Top management commitment will be fulfilled through joint board meetings and reviews. There will be a joint business plan, joint strategies, joint market research. Information flow should be streamlined, and information systems integration will be planned or in place. Transaction costs will be reduced and time will be taken out of work cycles. Billing will be bespoke to that buying company.

Graphically, the diamond is still the core shape of the relationship, but the lines have blurred (Figure 2.6). Focus teams, involving staff from both companies will be established to improve all aspects of joint company activity.

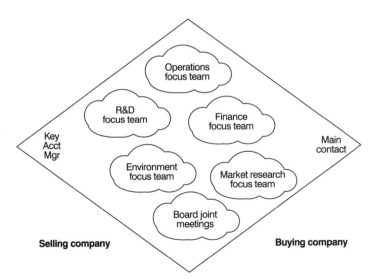

Figure 2.6 The Synergistic-KAM stage

> One manufacturer of capital goods built a factory close to a key account to maximize the potential for process integration.

> A logistics company, together with one of its retail key accounts, had six cross-boundary focus teams working on process improvement at any one time.

> A cleaning services company was quite used to the concept of its staff reporting to client managers. Everybody in the company had to do some boundary spanning. Even the most junior of staff on a contract would be specially trained in the key account's requirements.

A few general points can be noted about companies that have been successful in achieving synergistic relationships with key accounts:

- There is widespread understanding in the company that key account management is strategically right, and the determination exists at the highest level of the company to stick with it for the long term.
- The company has a comprehensive and meaningful recipe which distinguishes key accounts from non-key accounts, and takes notice of the customer's need for it as a supplier as well as vice versa.
- Key accounts have dedicated teams, or at least there is a wide understanding within the company of who the key accounts are and how they are to be treated.
- The company ensures that in terms of organization and processes, it is customer focused rather than internally focused – the more integrated supplier/customer processes become, the greater the potential for synergistic relationships.
- Patience and persistence are highly valued as well as dynamism, as sometimes it takes years to develop key accounts to synergistic levels.
- High status is attributed to key account managers, so that they have the incentive to stay and thus develop the account. Importance is also attributed to what other professionals achieve for key accounts.

These factors are discussed in more detail in later chapters.

Uncoupling-KAM

> Transactions and interactions cease.

There is a sixth stage in the relational development model that demands key account strategists' attention. It is worth exploring at length, because, by understanding the causes of uncoupling, we can reverse them and generate key account management success factors.

Uncoupling-KAM describes relational breakdown. Breakdowns can occur at any stage for a number of reasons. Many purchasing professionals might expect a selling company to sit down and discuss exit plans alongside any contract to supply. Exit plans have certainly been common in manufacturer/ retailer relationships. Even where exit plans are not formally required, it would be prudent to develop contingency plans for Uncoupling-KAM, if only to reduce the likelihood of it happening.

Some supplier/customer relationships are ill conceived and others are affected in a negative way by changes in the external environment and changes internal to one or both organizations. Uncoupling-KAM is rarely caused by price problems.

Interrelational causes of uncoupling

A change in key personnel
We have already commented on the risks associated with relying on only one point of contact. Relationships between the selling company organization and the buying company organization ought to operate at many levels. If relationships are not institutionalized, organization to organization, then the so-called 'single point of contact' personal relationship between the key account manager and his or her main contact will be all that holds the business together. If either leaves, the buying company is presented with an ideal switching point. Similarly, if the relationship between the two main contacts deteriorates for any reason and action is not taken, switching can occur which would be unlikely if there were links at many other points, including board level.

The list of examples of potential impetus for switching, which is linked to a single point of contact is long:

- A new key account manager is perceived to be less skilled than his or her predecessor.
- A new purchasing manager has a price-driven approach.
- The key account manager is off sick for an extended period and colleagues cannot provide adequate cover.
- The key account manager can never be contacted.
- The purchasing manager has to choose between two selling companies for single sourcing, and one loses the key account manager during the campaign.
- A popular key account manager is poached by a competitor.
- A change in one or other main contact results in a clash of personalities.
- One or other main contact is unwilling to share information.
- Due to recessionary pressures, a purchasing manager feels pressurized to push price negotiation too far.

- A purchasing manager objects to changes in key account managers being too frequent.
- A key account manager's level of service, ideas and frequency of contacts are vested in the individual and not general company culture.

If business and personal links are not forged at multiple levels, exit from special relationships is all too easy for either party's long-term interests. When relationships operate at more than one level, personal qualities can be assigned to the company – such as 'company X always employs nice people'.

'We rely a lot on the professionalism of our key account manager. If she were to leave, I think it would be very difficult for the supplier to replace her.'

A purchasing manager moving from a multisourcing to a single sourcing policy was having problems deciding between two suppliers of a certain commodity, both of whom seemed to be getting everything right. The key account manager of one company left, and so the purchasing manager vested all the business in the other supplier.

Breach of trust
A breach of trust is the one thing which has the potential to really kill a business relationship, although the stronger the relationship, the more forgiving it is likely to be of genuine mistakes. If, however, inconsistent performance is persistent, or a single event that is of overwhelming importance to the customer is handled badly, a breach of trust can be said to have occurred. For example when insurance companies sought government help to deal with claims after bombs in the City of London, buying companies perceived it as a disgraceful avoidance of responsibility. This affected relationships between the insurance companies and their customers.

Buying companies do not like shocks from selling companies. The best approach for a selling company about to miss a deadline, delivery or any other sort of routine obligation, is to let the customer know in advance. It is important, if something cannot be done, to say what cannot be done and why, and propose remedial action. The seriousness of the situation is multiplied when the customer is taken by surprise by the problem. It is subsequently fatal if the selling company fails to demonstrate any humility. Buying companies expect dealings with an important supplier to be fair. Trust involves appreciating the customer's point of view when something goes wrong, not abusing the privileged position of preferred supplier or brand leader.

A breach of trust is often rooted in a lack of communication. Selling companies know that they can always improve the information they disseminate to buying companies about what they are doing and why, as well as providing information about the customer's business from their viewpoint. Electronic data interchange and electronic mail can be instrumental in overcoming lack of communication in seller/buyer relationships.

Simple communication lapses within a selling company can be even more disappointing to a buying company, for example if credit control pursue a key account for a small debt. Buying companies who have been told that they are key accounts expect everyone in that supplier to know that they are a key account.

A food processing company had a problem with a supplier's ingredients that caused it to lose production. The technical manager called them in to discuss the matter and reported that they started banging the table, telling him that his staff could not have been using their product properly. Needless to say, that supplier was never used again.

A manufacturing company nearly broke off a partnership agreement with a raw materials supplier when it failed to deliver some product as promised, causing manufacturing delays. It was not so much that it had had a problem that annoyed the purchasing manager of the buying company, it was that no warning was given.

Exhaustion/lack of persistence

Selling companies may lose accounts through neglect. From time to time, key account activity needs revitalization. The longer a business relationship continues, the more difficult it is to sustain a high level of attention to its progress. Complacency and frustration can creep in, and partnership becomes a debased word.

'We overlooked the need to introduce our newest equipment to key accounts first, and some thought that we were taking them for granted.'

Cultural mismatch

Some companies have difficulty relating to others of a different culture. The main cultural mismatch mentioned is price versus value. A company who concentrates on price deals might still be a key account, but will be most likely to change hands, and therefore likely to have low status in the selling company. Meanwhile a company with modest market share but interested in partnership sourcing can increase its importance to a selling company.

There is also a perceived cultural gap between companies with a history of bureaucracy and those with entrepreneurial origins which has spawned a 'can do' culture with little regard for procedures. It is possible for partners to bridge the gap, but only where the importance of integral communications is well understood and applied.

National and regional cultures can create difficulties in doing business. Companies quite often struggle to find people with the skills to deal with differences across international boundaries.

Another manifestation of cultural mismatch is the fear of denigration of brand values. Suppliers with strong brands are loath to deal with buying companies who might not treat the brands with the respect the selling company feels is appropriate. Volume potential here may be offset against strategic considerations, or the relationship may be forced in order to comply with competition law.

'There's a certain arrogance about market leaders because they know you have to stock their brand. They should not take key accounts for granted ...'

'We know they come from a very bureaucratic background and they know we are very entrepreneurial. We have to be careful to make sure we learn from each other's culture rather than end up clashing.'

'I don't think they like buying from the British — we have to globalize!'

Quality problems

If a product or service fails to keep pace with competitors, or if the buying company experiences performance problems, the relationship with the selling company may be terminated. Process excellence, and high quality professional staff, are also expected from companies espousing key account management.

'The supplier of this machine just hasn't kept up with the market. When we come to replace it, other companies will have much better offers. We can't refuse to take better technology just because we like the account manager.'

Learning points

In order to ensure achievement with key accounts, we must reverse the potential causes of uncoupling to note the following success factors:

- Succession policy for key account managers must be carefully handled.
- Multifaceted communications and a spirit of mutual trust must be established at many levels across both organizations.
- Care must be taken to ensure that customer expectations are consistently met.
- Cultural challenges must be identified and, if appropriate and possible, overcome.
- Efforts must be made to inject dynamism into the relationship.
- The selling company must constantly achieve high levels of product, process and people quality.

External causes of uncoupling

Changing market positions
If a buying company suffers a dramatic loss of market share, key account management benefits do not seem so cost effective to the selling company. Certainly, the buying company that loses market share will no longer enjoy access to the top key account managers. They are very status conscious about their customers and would not want to stay on an account whose market share had shrunk.

'My account is losing market share because of problems following an acquisition. It is getting to the point where I want to transfer to another account.' Key account manager.

Financial problems
Some account relationships falter or are terminated when either party experiences financial problems.

Figure 2.7 provides a summary of the relational development model.

Analysing the potential for partnership/synergy

It is important for key account strategists in selling companies to establish whether or not a relationship between a supplier and customer can achieve higher relationship levels, and therefore would be suitable for a collaborative approach. An examination of the product/process mix, and value chain considerations can be helpful.

Pre-KAM	Early-KAM	Mid-KAM	Partnership-KAM	Synergistic-KAM	Uncoupling-KAM
Selling company seeks to establish interest in its product or service	Transactions commence	Selling company now one of a few 'preferred suppliers'	Selling company is now a strategic, possibly single source of supply	'Quasi-integration' – selling company and buying company together deliver value to the end customer	Relationship is suddenly broken off, or gradual deterioration causes buying company to invoke exit plans
Single point of contact likely	Single point of contact strengthened	Operational staff get to know their opposite numbers	Contacts at all levels	Focus teams at all interfaces between supplier and customer	

Figure 2.7 Tabular summary of the relational development model

The product/process mix

The potential for Synergistic-KAM largely depends on the correlation between the complexity of the processes between the selling company and buying company, and the complexity of the product and technology the selling company is delivering (Figure 2.8).

If both product and process are complex, optimum mutual benefit, and benefit for the end buying company, is obtained through some degree of vertical integration. The needs of the buying company are constantly evolving, and can be best fulfilled by a supplier with very detailed knowledge of the context in which it operates. This explains why partnership and synergistic relationships are usually observed in industrial and business-to-business markets.

Where there is a mix of simple and complex, there is potential for all levels of KAM to be represented in seller–buyer relationships. Bespoke services added to a common set of products and skills, together with intangibles such as brand leadership, innovation and professionalism, can be used as leverage for a key account management approach.

If both product and process are simple, it is more likely that relationships will remain 'transactional' and not move beyond the Early-KAM stage. The buying company's needs are very specific and easily defined. They are probably fulfilled by a commodity product that can be easily applied and easily sold, perhaps even over the Internet. This partially explains why relationships between some manufacturers of consumer goods and some retailers are traditionally adversarial.

However, it is not impossible for a company offering a commodity product or service to gain advantage from key account management. There are examples in the Cranfield research (McDonald, Millman and Rogers, 1996) of companies who assumed responsibility for some customer processes to gain single sourcing for a

Key account process

	Simple	Complex
Complex	Examples 1. Technical consultancy 2. Pharmaceuticals	Examples 1. Highly complex one-off manufactured goods 2. Bespoke information systems
Simple	Examples 1. Commodity electronics Fast-moving consumer goods	Examples 1. Customized financial services 2. Logistics

Product

Figure 2.8 The product/process matrix

commodity offering. The product core can always be clothed with services and intangibles that make it unique. Services that take hassle out of the customer's life can be particularly powerful, e.g. consignment stock, output-specified services.

KAM in the value chain context

In assessing the potential to achieve close, long-term relationships with buying companies, selling companies will always have to take into account the context in which the buying company operates. In addition to the product/process context, another key determinant affecting KAM approaches seems to be the positioning of the selling company/buying company dyad in the value chain. Figure 2.9 shows a very simple value chain.

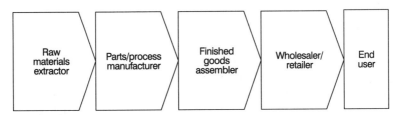

Figure 2.9 The value chain

> Manufacturers offer a great deal of potential for long-term partnerships. They are under considerable pressure on quality and partnership agreements with suppliers not only to deliver traceability, but also the potential for cross-boundary process redesign which will deliver added value further along the supply chain.

A partnership sourcing policy is often precipitated by the need for traceability in cases of product defects and the need to reduce administrative costs. Food and pharmaceutical manufacturers are particularly sensitive to traceability in raw materials, and the integrity of preferred suppliers is highly valued, even where alternative sources are deemed necessary. These industries are also perceived to be operating with high risks, and selling companies who can understand and can respond to that environment are valued. Honest advice is important. Standards of quality in all manufacturing plants are under constant pressure to improve.

> Retailers usually seem reluctant to offer their suppliers exclusivity or even preference. They perceive a powerful role for themselves in the value chain, as owners of the interface with the consumer.

Retailers are still key accounts to their selling companies, but even exceptional performance on meeting retailers' needs will not enable much ascendancy over the competition. Retailers would say that they were driven by consumers to provide choice. Consumers easily switch brands, and this is reflected in the purchasing style of retail organizations, which must provide them with the opportunity to switch.

The exception is where there is a brand leader in any one retail category. A manufacturer with a commanding value positioning with the consumer will meet the retailer on equal terms, but negotiations may still be adversarial. The professionalism of the key account manager will be expected to be high and the retailing purchasing professional is used to brand leader key account managers with high status, who can reduce hassle factors and deliver requirements. Nevertheless, the purchasing manager will still challenge any perceived over-use of a brand leadership position.

Despite all the additional challenges to partnership when the buying company is a retailer, the advantages that might be gained are being recognized. Retailers are beginning to explore aspects of partnership with selling companies. Their motivation is to manage categories (such as dairy, bakery, fresh meat, etc. in food retailing) to achieve the most profitable product mixes. The co-operation of suppliers, including added value such as merchandising or joint promotions, could contribute towards this objective.

Service suppliers may perceive opportunity for long-term partnerships in all parts of the value chain. This is particularly true where the service provided is completely outsourced to one company on a multiple year contract. Cleaning and catering are common examples of outsourced services, while information services outsourcing is becoming widespread. A long-term contract in itself does not provide the opportunity for partnership activity. Service providers in particular are likely to emphasize that value-based contracts, where selling company and buying company concentrate on delivering value to the end customer, are the prerequisite for partnership.

Achieving better process integration than a competitor, through joint teamwork, can be the next best thing to outsourcing.

A spirit of partnership, long-term commitment and a proactive approach can overcome the fact that any particular service may be a very small part of the buying company's overall expenses. The selling company that concentrates on reducing the buying company's hassle factors through key account management is creating competitive edge.

Global sourcing of materials, components, assemblies and equipment is common in the biggest manufacturing companies; but global sourcing of services is more difficult. Many services are traditionally concentrated in the small business sector, and there are few selling companies that can provide consistent service levels world wide. Those few are well placed to make global manufacturers their key accounts.

Subjective attitudes

In addition to the objective analyses that might be applied to assess potential for partnership, subjective attitudes must obviously be considered when selling company strategists assess how much to invest in developing a key account. Some buying companies have very positive views about partnerships with suppliers, some are avowedly adversarial and there are many shades in-between.

Summary

This chapter has:

- Examined the nature of the progression of key account relationships, with reference to the relational development model.
- Considered the possible reasons for the failure of relationships, and what can be learnt from that failure.
- Introduced preliminary analyses that can help a company to assess the potential for partnership in any particular relationship or market segment.

Quotes are drawn from real situations described by contributors to Cranfield's research into key account management.

Chapter 3

Key account planning in the context of strategic marketing planning

Introduction

The purpose of this chapter is to explain the key elements of marketing planning and to position key account planning in this context. It is in three sections: the first examines marketing planning myths; the second outlines the main steps involved in marketing planning; and the third looks briefly at the implementation and design of marketing planning systems and positions key account management within this process.

Wherever a key account is positioned on the relational development model, if a supplier has aspirations for building a relationship over time, some kind of plan setting out a strategy for how this is to be achieved will be necessary. The problem with this is that most organizations are not very good at, or even very knowledgeable about planning. In Chapter 5, we will explain how to prepare a strategic plan for a key account. This, however, must be placed firmly in the context of strategic marketing planning, otherwise it will not be effective. Most of this chapter, then, is about strategic marketing planning.

Marketing planning myths

Whatever the precise balance between the many underlying causes for the relative economic decline of nations within Western Europe, part of it can be explained by a poor understanding of marketing on the part of senior managers. However, when it comes to marketing planning, the widespread ignorance is of even greater concern. This conclusion is based on a four-year study carried out at Cranfield into how industrial goods companies selling internationally carry out their marketing planning.

> This survey showed that while all managers agree that it is logical to find some rational way of identifying objectives, to choose one or more of them based on the firm's distinctive competence, and then to schedule and cost out what has to be done to achieve the chosen objectives, 90 per cent of companies don't do this. Instead, they complete budgets and forecasts.

What most companies think of as planning systems are little more than forecasting and budgeting systems. These give impetus and direction to tackling the current operational problems of the business, but tend merely to project the current business unchanged into the future, something often referred to in management literature as 'tunnel vision'.

The successes enjoyed in the past were often the result of the easy marketability of products, and during periods of high economic prosperity there was little pressure on companies to do anything other than solve operational problems as they arose. Careful planning for the future seemed unnecessary. However, most companies today are experiencing difficulties precisely because of this lack of planning and there is a growing realization that survival and success in the future will come only from patient and meticulous planning and market preparation. This entails making a commitment to the future.

> Today, there is widespread awareness of lost market opportunities through unpreparedness and real confusion over what to do about it. It is hard not to conclude, therefore, that there is a strong relationship between these two problems and the systems most widely in use at present – i.e. sales forecasting and budgeting systems.

Marketing's contribution to business success in manufacturing, distribution or merchanting activities lies in its commitment to detailed analysis of future opportunities to meet customer needs and a wholly professional approach to selling to well-defined market segments those products or services that deliver the sought-after benefits. While prices and discounts are important, as are advertising and promotion, the link with operations through the product is paramount. But such a commitment and activities must not be mistaken for budgets and forecasts. Those, of course, we need and we have already got (our accounting colleagues have long since seen to that).

> Put quite bluntly, the process of marketing planning is concerned with identifying what and to whom and how sales are going to be made in the longer term to give revenue budgets and sales forecasts any chance of achievement.

Furthermore, chances of achievement are a function of how good our intelligence services are; how well suited are our strategies; and how well we are led.

Let us begin with a reminder of some of the basics. Marketing planning is a logical sequence and a series of activities leading to the setting of marketing objectives and the formulation of plans for achieving them. It is a management process. Conceptually, the process is very simple. Marketing planning by means of a planning system is, *per se*, little more than a structured way of identifying a range of options for the company, of making them explicit in writing, of formulating marketing objectives which are consistent with the company's overall objectives, and of scheduling and costing out the specific activities most likely to bring about the achievement of the objective. It is being systematic with this process which is distinctive and which lies at the heart of the theory of marketing planning and which delivers the following benefits:

- co-ordination of the activities of many individuals whose actions are interrelated over time;
- identification of expected developments;
- preparedness to meet changes when they occur;
- minimization of non-rational responses to the unexpected;
- better communication among executives; and
- minimization of conflicts among individuals which would result in a subordination of the goals of the company to those of the individual.

Operational problems resulting from the forecasting and budgeting approach

The following are the most frequently mentioned operating problems resulting from a reliance on traditional sales forecasting and budgeting procedures in the absence of a marketing planning system:

- lost opportunities for profit;
- meaningless numbers in long-range plans;
- unrealistic objectives;
- lack of actionable market information;
- interfunctional strife;
- management frustration;

- proliferation of products and markets;
- wasted promotional expenditure;
- pricing confusion;
- growing vulnerability to environmental change; and
- loss of control over the business.

It is not difficult to see the connection between all of these problems. Nor is it difficult to see that strategic planning for key accounts is unlikely to be effective given the disorganized state of the supplying company. However, what is perhaps not apparent from the list is that each of these operational problems is in fact a symptom of a much larger problem that emanates from the way in which the objectives of a firm are set.

> Sales targets for the sales force are often inflated in order to motivate them to higher achievement, while the actual budgets themselves are deflated in order to provide a safety net against shortfall.

Both act as demotivators and both lead to the frequent use of expressions such as 'ritual', 'the numbers game', 'meaningless horse trading', and so on. It is easy to see how the problems listed above begin to manifest themselves in this sort of environment.

Closely allied to this is the frequent reference to profit as being the only objective necessary for successful business performance. There is in the minds of many business people the assumption that in order to be commercially successful, all that is necessary is for the 'boss' to set profit targets, to decentralize the firm into groups of similar activities and then to make managers accountable for achieving those profits.

> Even though many companies in Western Europe made the making of 'profit' almost their sole objective, many of their industries have gone into decline, and ironically, there has also been a decline in real profitability.

Overall volume increases and minimum rates of return on investment are frequently applied to all products and markets, irrespective of market share, market growth rate, or the longevity of the product life cycle. Indeed there is a lot of evidence to show that many companies are in trouble today precisely because their decentralized units manage their business only for the current profit and loss account, often at the expense of giving up valuable and hard-earned market share, failing to invest in research and development, and running down the current business.

> Financial objectives, while being essential measures of the desired performance of a company, are of little practical help, since they say nothing about how the results are to be achieved.

The same applies to sales forecasts and budgets, which are not marketing objectives and strategies. Understanding the real meaning and significance of marketing objectives helps managers to know what information they need to enable them to think through the implications of choosing one or more positions in the market. Finding the right words to describe the logic of marketing objectives and strategies is infinitely more difficult than writing down numbers on a piece of paper and leaving the strategies implicit. This lies at the heart of the problem. For clearly, a number-oriented system will not encourage managers to think in a structured way about strategically relevant market segments, nor will it encourage the collection, analysis and synthesis of actionable market data. And in the absence of such activities within operating units, it is unlikely that headquarters will have much other than intuition and 'feel' to use as a basis for decisions about the management of scarce resources.

Later in this book, we will describe the process for managing complex relationships with key accounts. Already, however, it will be clear that without a more sensible corporate approach to strategic marketing planning, not even the very best of key account managers would be able to manage strategies for building long-term profitable relationships.

How can these problems be overcome?

One of the main difficulties is how to get managers throughout an organization to think beyond the horizon of the current year's operations. This applies universally to all types and sizes of company. Even chief executives of small companies find difficulty in breaking out of the fetters of the current profit and loss account, so it is easy to see why suppliers still have difficulty thinking and planning strategically for key accounts.

> The problem, particularly in large companies, is that managers who are evaluated and rewarded on the basis of current operations find difficulty in concerning themselves about the corporate future.

This is exacerbated by behavioural issues in the sense that it is safer, and more rewarding personally, for managers to do what they know best, which in most cases is to manage their current range of products and customers in order to make the current year's budget.

Events that affect economic performance in a business come from so many directions, and in so many forms, that it is impossible for any manager to be precise about how to interact in the form of problems to be overcome, and opportunities to be exploited. The best a manager can do is to form a reasoned view about how they have affected the past, and how they will develop in the future, and what action needs to be taken over a period of time to enable the company to prepare itself for the expected changes. The problem is how to get managers to formulate their thoughts about these things, for until they have, it is unlikely that any objectives that are set will have much relevance or meaning.

Accordingly, they need some system that will help them to think in a structured way about problem formulation. It is the provision of such a rational framework to help them to make explicit their intuitive economic models of the business that is almost totally lacking from the forecasting and budgeting systems of most companies. It is apparent that in the absence of any such synthesized and simplified views of the business, setting meaningful objectives for the future seems like an insurmountable problem, and this in turn encourages the perpetuation of systems involving merely the extrapolation of numbers.

There is also substantial evidence that those companies that provide procedures for this process, however informal, have gone some considerable way to overcoming the problem.

To summarize, a structured approach to situation analysis is necessary, irrespective of the size or complexity of the organization. Such a system should:

- ensure that comprehensive consideration is given to the definition of strengths and weaknesses and to problems and opportunities;
- ensure that a logical framework is used for the presentation of the key issues arising from this analysis.

Very few companies in the Cranfield study had planning systems that possessed these characteristics. Those that did managed to cope with their environment more effectively than those that did not. They found it easier to set meaningful marketing objectives, were more confident about the future, enjoyed greater control over the business, and reacted less on a piecemeal basis to ongoing events. In short, they suffered less operational problems and were, as a result, more effective organizations.

The strategic marketing planning process

It is clear, therefore, that strategic marketing planning is essential when we consider the increasingly hostile and complex environment in which companies operate. Hundreds of external and internal factors interact in a bafflingly complex way to affect our ability to achieve profitable sales. Managers of a company have to have some understanding or view about how all these variables interact and managers try to be rational about their business decisions, no matter how important intuition and experience may be.

> Most managers accept that some kind of formalized procedure for marketing planning helps reduce the complexity of business operations and adds a dimension of realism to the company's hopes for the future.

The steps

The steps described here are exactly the same as the steps required to produce a strategic plan for a key account. This is described in more detail in Chapter 5.

Figure 3.1 illustrates the several stages that have to be gone through in order to arrive at a strategic marketing plan, and highlights the difference between the process of marketing planning and the actual plan itself, which is the output of the process (shown in the box in Figure 3.1).

Each of the stages illustrated in Figure 3.1, starting with the marketing audit, will be discussed in more detail later in this chapter. The dotted lines joining up

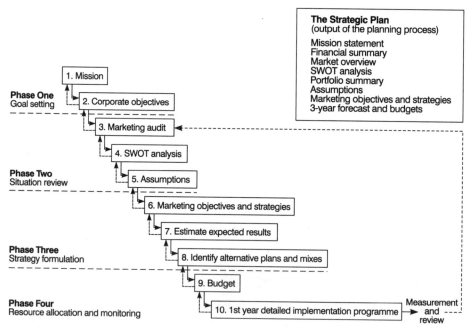

Figure 3.1 The strategic marketing planning process

the steps are meant to indicate the reality of the planning process, in that it is likely that each of these steps will have to be gone through more than once before final programmes can be written.

Where marketing planning has failed, it has generally been because companies have placed too much emphasis on the procedures themselves and the resulting paperwork, rather than on generating information useful to, and consumable by, management. Also, where companies relegate marketing planning to someone called a 'planner' it invariably fails, for the single reason that planning for line management cannot be delegated to a third party.

> The real role of the 'planner' should be to help those responsible for implementation to plan. Failure to recognize this simple fact can be disastrous.

Finally, planning failures often result from companies trying too much, too quickly, and without training staff in the use of procedures.

We can now look at the strategic marketing planning process in more detail, starting with a look at the marketing audit. So far we have looked at the need for marketing planning and outlined a series of steps that have to be gone through in order to arrive at a marketing plan. However, any plan will only be as good as the information on which it is based, and the marketing audit is the means by which information for planning is organized, something which will become clear in respect of key account planning discussed in Chapter 5.

What is a marketing audit?

Auditing as a process is usually associated with the financial side of a business and is conducted according to a defined set of accounting standards, which are well documented, easily understood, and which therefore lend themselves readily to the auditing process. The total business process, although more complicated, innovative and relying more on judgement than on a set of rules, is still nevertheless capable of being audited.

> An audit is a systematic, critical and unbiased review and appraisal of the environment and of the company's operations. A marketing audit is part of the larger management audit and is concerned with the marketing environment and marketing operations.

When you come to Chapter 5 you will see how an individual audit needs to be carried out for each key account.

Why is there a need for an audit?

Often the need for an audit does not manifest itself until things start to go wrong for a company, such as falling sales and margins, lost market share, and so on. At times like these, management often attempts to treat the wrong symptoms, the most frequent result of which is to reorganize the company! But such measures are unlikely to be effective if there are more fundamental problems that have not been identified. Of course, if the company could survive long enough, it might eventually solve its problems through a process of elimination! Essentially, the argument is that problems have to be properly defined, and the audit is a means of helping to define them.

To summarize, the audit is a structured approach to the collection and analysis of information and data in the complex business environment and is an essential prerequisite to problem solving.

The form of the audit

Any company carrying out an audit will be faced with two kinds of variables. First, there are variables over which the company has no direct control. These usually take the form of what can be described as environmental and market variables. Second, there are variables over which the company has complete control. These we can call operational variables. This provides a clue as to how we can structure an audit. That is to say, in two parts, external audit, and internal audit. The external audit is concerned with the uncontrollable variables such as the economy and the market served by the company, while the internal audit is concerned with the controllable variables, which are usually the firm's internal resources. The panel below contains a checklist of areas that should be investigated as part of the marketing audit. Each one of these headings will need to be examined with a view to building up an information base relevant to the company's performance.

When should the audit be carried out?

A mistaken belief held by many people is that the marketing audit should be some kind of final attempt to define a company's marketing problem, or at best something done by an independent body from time to time to ensure that a company is on the right lines.

However, since marketing is such a complex function, it seems illogical not to carry out a pretty thorough situation analysis at least once a year at the beginning of the planning cycle.

The marketing audit checklist

External audit

Business and economic environment

- Economic
- Political/fiscal/legal
- Social/cultural
- Technological
- Intracompany

The Market
- Total market, size, growth and trends (value/volume)
- Market characteristics, developments and trends
  - Products
  - Prices
  - Physical distribution
  - Channels
  - Customers/consumers
  - Communication
  - Industry practices

Competition
- Major competitors
- Size
- Market shares/coverage
- Market standing/reputation
- Production capabilities
- Distribution policies
- Marketing methods
- Extent of diversification
- Personnel issues
- International links
- Profitability
- Key strengths and weaknesses

Internal audit

Marketing operational variables (own company)

- Sales (total, by geographical location, by industrial type, by customer, by product)
- Market shares
- Profit margins/costs
- Marketing information/research
- Marketing mix variables as follows:
  - Product management
  - Price
  - Distribution
  - Promotion
  - Operations and resources

There is much evidence to show that many highly successful companies, as well as using normal information and control procedures and marketing research throughout the year, also start their planning cycle each year with a formal review (through an audit-type process) of everything that has had an important influence on marketing activities. Certainly in many leading consumer goods companies, the annual self-audit approach is a tried and tested discipline integrated into the management process.

Who should carry out the audit?

Occasionally it may be justified to hire outside consultants to carry out a marketing audit to check that a company is getting the most out of its resources. However, it seems an unnecessary expense to have this done every year.

The answer, therefore, is to have an audit carried out annually by the company's own line managers on their own areas of responsibility.

Objections to this usually revolve around the problems of time and objectivity. In practice, these problems are overcome by institutionalizing procedures so that all managers have to conform to a disciplined approach, and secondly by thorough training in the use of the procedures themselves. However, even this will not result in achieving the purpose of an audit unless a rigorous discipline is applied from the highest down to the lowest levels of management involved in the audit. Such a discipline is usually successful in helping managers to avoid the sort of tunnel vision that often results from a lack of critical appraisal.

What happens to the results of the audit?

The only remaining question is what happens to the results of the audit? Some companies consume valuable resources carrying out audits that bring very little by way of actionable results. There is a mistaken belief that a marketing audit is a marketing plan. But, it isn't. It is just a database that has been translated into relevant information.

> The task remains of turning the marketing audit into intelligence, which is information that is essential for making decisions. This intelligence, or knowledge, will be the strategic marketing plan for a period of about three years.

Since the objective of the audit is to indicate what a company's marketing objectives and strategies should be, it follows that it would be helpful if some format could be found for organizing the major findings.

One useful way of doing this is in the form of a number of SWOT analyses. This is a summary of the audit under the headings, internal strengths and weaknesses as they relate to external opportunities and threats. Each SWOT analysis should, if possible, contain not more than four or five paragraphs of commentary focusing on key factors only. It should highlight internal differential strengths and weaknesses *vis-à-vis* competitors and key external opportunities and threats. A summary of reasons for good or bad performance should be included. It should be interesting to read, contain concise statements, include only relevant and important data, and give emphasis to creative analysis.

These SWOT analyses will be a central part of the strategic marketing plan, as will the other elements listed below. The strategic marketing plan should include the following:

Mission statement

The mission statement should state clearly:

- the role or purpose of the business unit being planned for;
- its business definition;
- its distinctive competence;
- future indications in the form of what it will, might and will never do.

A financial summary

This is obviously done last, but appears here. It is like an Executive Summary.

Market overview

Start with a market overview:

- what is the market?
- how does it work?
- has the market declined or grown?
- how does it break down into segments?
- what is your share of each?

Keep it simple; if you do not have the facts, make estimates. Use market maps, life cycles, portfolios, bar charts, pie charts and so on to make it all crystal clear.

SWOT analyses

Now identify the key segments for you, and do a SWOT for each one:

- list the key factors for success;
- outline the major outside influences and their impact on each segment;
- give an assessment of your company's strengths and weaknesses vis-à-vis competitors.

Highlight differential strengths and weaknesses, and

- give an explanation for good or bad performance.

Portfolio summary (of the SWOTS)

Now plot each of your major segments on which you have completed a SWOT onto a directional policy matrix showing the relative market attractiveness of each on the vertical axis and your relative strengths in each market on the horizontal axis. (This will be explained in more detail in the next chapter.)

Assumptions

Assumptions now have to be made.

There are certain key determinants of success in all companies about which assumptions have to be made before the planning process can proceed. It is really a question of standardizing the planning environment. For example it would be no good receiving plans from two product managers, one of whom believed the market was going to increase by 10 per cent, while the other believed the market was going to decline by 10 per cent.

Examples of assumptions might be: with respect to the company's industrial climate, it is assumed that:

1 Industrial overcapacity will increase from 105 per cent to 115 per cent as new industrial plants come into operation.
2 Price competition will force price levels down by 10 per cent across the board.
3 A new product in the field of x will be introduced by our major competitor before the end of the second quarter.

> Assumptions should be few in number, and if a plan is possible irrespective of the assumptions made, then the assumptions are unnecessary.

Marketing objectives and strategies

The next step in marketing planning is the writing of marketing objectives and strategies, the key stage in the whole process – if this is not done properly, everything that follows is of little value.

This is an obvious activity to follow on with, since a thorough situation review, particularly in the area of marketing, should enable the company to determine whether it will be able to meet the long-range financial targets with its current range of products in its current markets. Any projected gap can be filled by the various methods of product development, market extension, or a combination of both, as shown in Figure 3.2.

We discuss below marketing objectives and strategies in more detail. For now, the important point to make is that this is the time in the planning cycle when a compromise has to be reached between what is wanted by the several functional departments and what is practicable, given all the constraints that

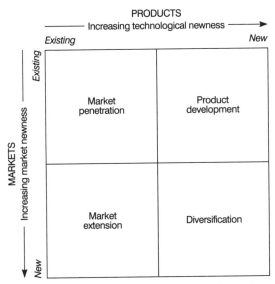

Figure 3.2 Marketing objectives and strategies (the Ansoff matrix)

any company has. For example it is no good setting a marketing objective of penetrating a new market if the company does not have the production capacity to cope with the new business, and if capital is not available for whatever investment is necessary in additional capacity. At this stage, objectives and strategies will be set for three years, or for whatever the planning horizon is.

An objective is what you want to achieve. A strategy is how you plan to achieve your objectives.

Thus, there can be objectives and strategies at all levels in marketing, for example advertising objectives and strategies and pricing objectives and strategies.

However, the important point to remember about marketing objectives is that they are about products and markets only, i.e. what you sell and to whom.

Common sense will confirm that it is only by selling something to someone that the company's financial goals can be achieved, and that advertising, pricing, service levels, and so on are the means (or strategies) by which we might succeed in doing this. Thus, pricing objectives, sales promotion objectives, advertising objectives and the like should not be confused with marketing objectives.

Marketing objectives are simply about one or more of the following:

- existing products in existing markets;
- new products or existing markets;
- existing products for new markets; and
- new products for new markets.

They should be capable of measurement, otherwise they are not objectives.

Directional terms such as 'maximize', 'minimize', 'penetrate', 'increase', etc. are only acceptable if quantitative measurement can be attached to them.

Measurement should be in terms of sales volume, value, market share, profit, percentage penetration of outlets, and so on.

Marketing strategies are the means by which marketing objectives will be achieved and generally are concerned with 'the four Ps', as follows:

- *Product*: the general policies for product deletions, modifications, additions, design, packaging, etc.
- *Price*: the general pricing policies to be followed for product groups in market segments.
- *Place*: the general policies for channels and customer service levels.
- *Promotion*: the general policies for communicating with customers under the relevant headings, such as advertising, sales force, sales promotion, public relations, exhibitions, direct mail, etc.

Estimate expected results and identify alternative plans and mixes

Having completed this major task, it is normal at this stage to employ judgement, analogous experience, field tests, and so on, to test out the feasibility of the objectives and strategies in terms of market share, sales, costs, profits, and so on. It is also normally at this stage that alternative plans and mixes are discussed if necessary. It is a matter of judgement whether the options considered are included.

The budget

It is now possible to commit to a budget for the planning period (say, for three years).

The one-year marketing plan and budget

The general marketing strategies are now developed into specific sub-objectives, each supported by more detailed strategy and action statements for the first year of the strategic marketing plan.

A company organized according to functions might have an advertising plan, a sales promotion plan, a pricing plan, and so on. A product-based company might have a product plan, with objectives, strategies and tactics for price, place and promotion as necessary.

A market- or geographically based company might have a market plan, with objectives, strategies and tactics for the four Ps as necessary. Likewise, a company with a few major customers might have a customer plan. Any combination of the above might be suitable, depending on circumstances.

A written strategic marketing plan is the backcloth against which operational decisions are taken on an ongoing basis. Consequently too much detail should not be attempted. Its major function is to determine where the company is now, where it wants to go to, and how it intends to get there. It is at the heart of a company's revenue-generating activities and from it flows all other corporate activities, such as the timing of cash flows, the size and character of the labour force, and so on.

The strategic marketing plan should be distributed on a 'need to know' basis only and used as an aid to effective management. It cannot be a substitute for it.

It will be obvious from all of this that the setting of one-year budgets becomes not only much easier, but the resulting budgets are more likely to be realistic and related to what the whole company wants to achieve rather than just one functional department.

The problem of designing a dynamic system for budget setting rather than the 'tablets of stone' approach, which is more common, is a major challenge to the marketing and financial directors of all companies.

> The most satisfactory approach would be for marketing directors to justify all their marketing expenditure from a zero base each year against the tasks they wish to accomplish.

A little thought will confirm that this is exactly the approach recommended in this chapter. If these procedures are followed, a hierarchy of objectives is built up in such a way that every item of budgeted expenditure can be related directly back to the initial corporate financial objectives. For example if sales promotion is a major means of achieving an objective in a particular market, when sales promotional items appear in the programme, each one has a specific purpose which can be related back to a major objective.

Doing it this way not only ensures that every item of expenditure is fully accounted for as part of a rational, objective and task approach, but also that when changes have to be made during the financial year, such changes can be made in such a way that the least damage is caused to the company's long-term objectives.

In the detailed one-year plan, the incremental marketing expense can be considered to be all costs that are incurred after the product leaves the factory, other than costs involved in physical distribution, the costs of which usually represent a discrete subset. There is, of course, no textbook answer to problems relating to questions such as whether packaging should be a marketing or a product expense, and whether some distribution costs could be considered to be marketing costs. For example insistence on high service levels results in high inventory-carrying costs. Only common sense will reveal workable solutions to issues such as these.

Under price, however, any form of discounting that reduces the expected gross income, such as promotional discounts, quantity discounts, overriders and so on, as well as sales commission and unpaid invoices, should be given the most careful attention as incremental marketing expenses. Most obvious incremental marketing expenses will occur, however, under the heading 'promotion' in the form of advertising, sales force salaries and expenses, sales promotional expenditure, direct mail costs, and so on.

The important point about the measurable effects of marketing activity is that anticipated levels should be the result of the most careful analysis of what is required to take the company towards its goals, while the most careful attention should be paid to gathering all items of expenditure under appropriate headings. The healthiest way of treating these issues is a zero-based budgeting approach.

Marketing planning systems

Some indication of the potential complexity of marketing planning can be seen in Figure 3.3. Even in a generalized model such as this, it can be seen that in a large diversified group operating in many foreign markets, a complex combination of product, market and functional plans is possible. For example what is required at regional level will be different from what is required at headquarters level, while it is clear that the total corporate plan has to be built from the individual building blocks. Furthermore, the function of marketing itself may be further functionalized for the purpose of planning, such as marketing research, advertising, selling, distribution, promotion and so forth, while different customer groups may merit having separate plans drawn up. It will be observed that key account plans have not been included in this model, although it will be obvious that key account planning could be necessary not only at segment level, but at all levels indicated in Figure 3.3.

A number of points concerning requisite planning levels seem clear.

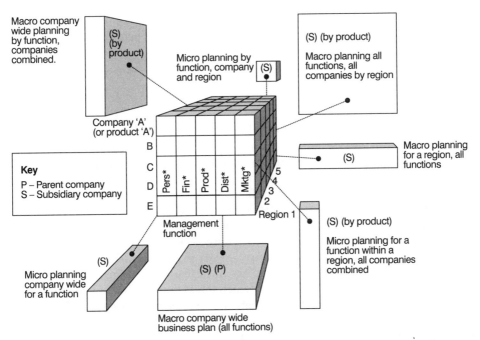

Figure 3.3 Macro business plan: all functions, all companies, all regions, together with constituent building blocks

First, in a large diversified group, irrespective of such organizational issues, anything other than a systematic approach approximating to a formalized marketing planning system is unlikely to enable the necessary control to be exercised over the corporate identity.

The results of planning

There can, however, be a problem with this. Creativity cannot flourish in an overly bureaucratic, formalized system. There would be little disagreement that in today's abrasive, turbulent and highly competitive environment, it is those firms that succeed in extracting entrepreneurial ideas and creative marketing programmes from systems that are necessarily yet acceptably formalized, that will succeed in the long run. Much innovative flair can so easily be stifled by systems. Certainly there is ample evidence of international companies with highly formalized systems that produce stale and repetitive plans, with little changed from year to year, that fail to point up the really key strategic issues as a result. The scandalous waste this implies is largely due to a lack of personal intervention by key managers during the early stages of the planning cycle.

> There is clearly a need, therefore, to find a way of perpetually renewing the planning life cycle each time around. Inertia must never set in. Without some such valve or means of opening up the loop, inertia quickly produces decay.

Such a valve has to be inserted early in the planning cycle during the audit, or situation review stage. In companies with effective marketing planning systems, whether such systems are formalized or informal, the critical intervention of senior managers – from the chief executive down through the hierarchical chain – comes at the draft plan stage. Essentially what takes place is a personalized presentation of preliminary findings, together with proposed marketing objectives, strategies and outline budgets for the strategic planning period. These are discussed, amended where necessary, and agreed in various synthesized formats at the hierarchical levels in the organization before any detailed operational planning takes place. It is at such meetings that managers are called upon to justify their views, which tends to force them to be more bold and creative than they would have been had they been allowed merely to send in their proposals.

Obviously, however, even here much depends on the degree to which managers take a critical stance, which is likely to be much greater when the chief executive takes an active part in the process. Every hour of time devoted at this stage by the chief executive has a multiplier effect throughout the remainder of the process. And it should be remembered we are not talking about budgets at this juncture, in anything other than outline form.

The marketing planning cycle and time horizons

It is crucial for key account managers to understand their role in the planning cycle. The schedule should call for work on the plan for the next year to begin early enough in the current year to permit adequate time for market research and analysis of key data and market trends. In addition, the plan should provide for the early development of a strategic plan that can be approved or altered in principle.

An important factor in determining the planning cycle is bound to be the degree to which it is practicable to extrapolate from sales and market data.

> Generally speaking, successful planning companies start the planning cycle formally somewhere between nine and six months from the beginning of the next fiscal year. It is not necessary to be constrained to work within the company's fiscal year.

It is quite possible to have a separate marketing planning schedule if that is appropriate, and simply organize the aggregation of results at the time required by the corporate financial controller.

One- and three-year planning periods are by far the most common. Lead time for the initiation of major new product innovations, the length of time necessary to recover capital investment costs, the continuing availability of customers and raw materials, and the size and usefulness of existing plant and buildings, are the most frequently mentioned reasons for having a three-year planning horizon. Many companies, however, do not give sufficient thought to what represents a sensible planning horizon for their particular circumstances. A five-year timespan is clearly too long for some companies, particularly those with highly versatile machinery operating in volatile fashion-conscious markets. The effect of this is to rob strategic plans of reality. A three-year horizon is often chosen largely because of its universality. Some small subsidiaries in large conglomerates are often asked to produce strategic plans for seven, ten and sometimes fifteen years ahead, with the result that they tend to become meaningless exercises.

> The conclusion to be reached is that there is a natural point of focus into the future beyond which it is pointless to look.

This point of focus is a function of the relative size of a company. Small companies, because of their size and the way they are managed, tend to be comparatively flexible in the way in which they can react to environmental turbulence in the short term. Large companies, on the other hand, need a much longer lead time in which to make changes in direction. Consequently, they tend to need to look further into the future and to use formalized systems for this purpose, so that managers throughout the organization have a common means of communication.

Positioning of marketing planning

There is one other major aspect to be considered. It concerns the requisite location of the marketing planning activity in a company.

> In the first instance, marketing planning should take place as near to the marketplace as possible, but such plans should then be reviewed at high levels within an organization to see what issues, if any, have been overlooked.

Because, in anything but the smallest of undiversified companies, it is not possible for top management to set detailed objectives for operating units, strategic guidelines are often issued at the beginning of the planning cycle. One way of doing this is in the form of a 'strategic planning letter'. Another is by means of a personal briefing by the chief executive at 'kick-off' meetings. These guidelines would proceed from the broad to the specific, and become more detailed as they progress through the company towards operating units. These guidelines are often under the headings of 'financial', 'manpower and organization', 'operations', and, of course, 'marketing'.

Under marketing, for example at the highest level in a large group, top management may ask for particular attention to be paid to issues such as the technical impact of microprocessors on electromechanical component equipment, leadership and innovation strategies, vulnerability to attacks from the flood of Far Eastern products, and so on. At operating company level, it is possible to be more explicit about target markets, product development, and the like.

Having carefully explained the point about requisite marketing planning, Figure 3.4 illustrates the principles by which the process should be implemented in any company. It shows a hierarchy of audits, SWOT analyses, objectives, strategies and programmes.

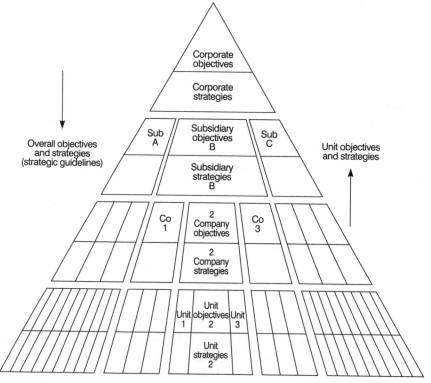

Figure 3.4 Strategic and operational planning – the hierarchy

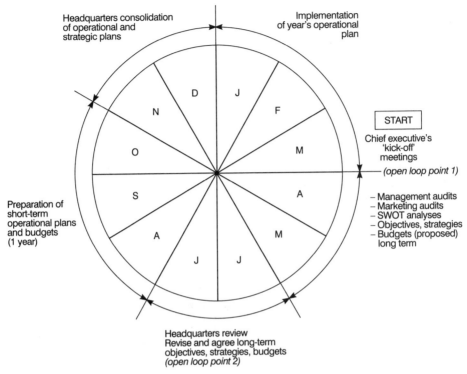

Figure 3.5 Strategic and operational planning – timing

Figure 3.5 is another way of illustrating the total corporate strategic and planning process. This time, however, a time element is added, and the relationship between strategic planning letters, long-term corporate plans and short-term operational plans is clarified. It is important to note that there are two 'open loop' points in Figure 3.5. These are the key times in the planning process when a subordinate's views and findings should be subjected to the closest examination by their superior. It is by taking these opportunities that marketing planning can be transformed into the critical and creative process it is supposed to be, rather than the dull, repetitive ritual it so often turns out to be. Figures 3.4 and 3.5 should be seen as one group of illustrations showing how the marketing planning process fits into the wider context of corporate planning.

The position of key account planning in the cycle

There is much debate about this, but it will be clear from looking at the planning cycle in Figure 3.5 that key account planning must take place at the same time as, or even before, draft plans are prepared for a strategic business unit.

If this is not clear, let us give an example of a supplies company servicing the needs of a national health service.

It will be seen there are four 'markets' within hospitals to be served. These are:

- Medical;
- Administration;
- Catering;
- Energy.

There will be a number of key accounts, or hospital groups, referred to here as Hospital Groups A, B, C, D, etc. Each of these hospital groups may well have their own key account manager who has to plan for them. Figure 3.6 illustrates this.

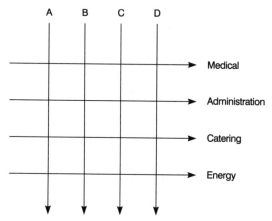

Figure 3.6 Hospital groups and key account managers

Thus, for example the key account manager for Hospital A has to prepare a draft plan across all four 'markets' and this would clearly be a key input to the planning process shown in Figure 3.5.

The position of key account planning in strategic marketing planning

Earlier, we stated that planning should start in the market where the customers are. Indeed, in anything other than small organizations, it is clearly absurd to think that any kind of meaningful planning can take place without the committed inputs of those who operate where the customers are.

Corporate plan					
Marketing plan					
Segment plan		Segment plan		Segment plan	
Account plan I	Account plan 2	Account plan 3	Account plan 4	Account plan 5	Account plan 6

Figure 3.7 The planning hierarchy

Figure 3.7 shows a hierarchy of planning starting with key account planning. Every principle outlined in this chapter applies right down to the individual key account. Thus, the planning process shown in Figure 3.5 would start with key accounts, so from this point onwards, the strategic and tactical planning focus turns to key accounts, for these are the main focus of this book.

Chapter 4

Identifying and targeting key accounts

Introduction

One of the objectives of this chapter is to place key account management in the context of market segmentation, for it is creative market segmentation that is universally recognized as the key to sustainable competitive advantage. Another is to provide a methodology for identifying and targeting key accounts, using account portfolio management. Finally, the difficult issue of how profits are made from key accounts is discussed.

Market segmentation

For most organizations, their different market segments will have in each of them a number of key accounts. Before categorizing key accounts, analysing their needs and then setting objectives and strategies, it is necessary to ensure that we have the clearest understanding of how our market works, what the key segments are and where we can bring the most influence to bear on decision making about what is bought and from whom. This is essential knowledge for it will be the backcloth against which plans for key accounts are evaluated and eventually controlled. Indeed, we will go so far as to say that an appreciation of market segmentation is an essential skill for effective key account management.

Market segmentation is the means by which any company seeks to gain a differential advantage over its competitors.

Markets usually fall into natural groups, or segments, which contain customers who exhibit the same broad characteristics. These segments form separate markets in themselves and can often be of considerable size. Taken to its extreme, each individual consumer is a unique market segment, for all people are different in their requirements.

However, it is clearly uneconomical to make unique products for the needs of individuals, except in the most unusual circumstances. Consequently, products are made to appeal to groups of customers who share approximately the same needs.

It is not surprising, then, to hear that there are certain universally accepted criteria concerning what constitutes a viable market segment:

- Segments should be of an adequate size to provide the company with the desired return for its effort.
- Members of each segment should have a high degree of similarity, yet be distinct from the rest of the market.
- Criteria for describing segments must be relevant to the purchase situation.
- Segments must be reachable.

While many of these criteria are obvious when we consider them, in practice market segmentation is one of the most difficult of marketing concepts to turn into a reality. Yet we must succeed, otherwise we become just another company selling what are called 'me too' products. In other words, what we offer the potential customer is very much the same as what any other company offers and, in such circumstances, it is likely to be the lowest priced article that is bought. This can be ruinous to our profits, unless we happen to have low costs, hence higher margins, than our competitors.

There are basically three steps to market segmentation, all of which have to be completed.

The first is essentially a manifestation of the way customers actually behave in the marketplace and consists of answering the question, who is buying what? The second answers the question why are they buying what they buy? The third step involves searching for market segments.

Market mapping

A useful way of tackling the complex issue of market segmentation is to start by drawing a 'market map' as a precursor to a more detailed examination of who buys what.

A market map defines the value chain between supplier and final user, which takes into account the various buying mechanisms found in a market, including the part played by 'influencers'. The more key account managers understand about the dynamics of their market, the more value they will be to the key accounts they are trying to add value to. Indeed, the Cranfield research showed that industry knowledge is highly valued by key accounts. This section, then, is intended to summarize this complex aspect of marketing management.

In general, if an organization's products or services go through the same channels to similar end users, one composite market map can be drawn. If, however, some products or services go through totally different channels and/ or to totally different markets, there will be a need for more than one market map.

It is probably sensible to treat different business units individually because such structures usually exist because the volume or value of business justifies such a specific focus. For example in the case of a farming co-operative supplying seeds, fertilizer, crop protection, insurance and banking to farmers, it would be sensible to start, initially, by drawing a separate market map for each of these product groups, even though they all appear to go through similar channels to the same end users. In the organization concerned, each one is treated as a separate business unit.

In other words, it is recommended that you start the mapping (and subsequent segmentation) process at the lowest level of disaggregation within the organization's current structure.

An example of a very basic market map is shown in Figure 4.1. It is very important that your market map tracks your products/services, along with those of your competitors, all the way through to the final user, even though you may not actually sell to them direct.

In some markets, the direct customer/purchaser will not always be the final user. For example a company (or household) may commission a third party contractor to carry out some redecoration, or an advertising agency to develop and conduct a promotional campaign, or a bank/accountant/financial adviser to produce and implement a financial programme. For all of us, the doctor we visit when seeking treatment is, in many respects, a contractor when it comes to prescribing medicine. Although the contractor is strictly the direct buyer, he or she is not the final user. The distinction is important because, to win the

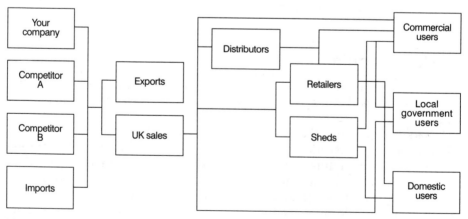

Figure 4.1 A simple market map

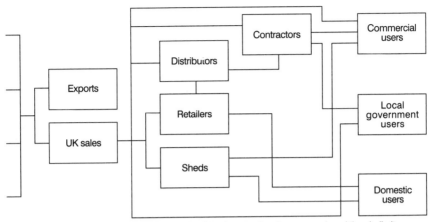

Note: In this particular market map the introduction of contractors has now reduced the similarity between the domestic and business-to-business end users quite notably. Sheds continue to be shared with a proportion of the commercial users, but this new contractor stage only operates in the business-to-business field.

Figure 4.2 Market map with contractor

commission, the contractor would have needed to understand the requirements of the customer and, in carrying out the commission, would have carried out those requirements on behalf of the customer. To miss out the final user from the market map would, therefore, have ignored an array of different needs which the supplier would need to be aware of (and have included in their product offer) if the supplier were to ensure the company name appeared on the contractor's 'preferred supplier list'. The inclusion of a contractor on a market map is illustrated in Figure 4.2.

As the figures have illustrated, most market maps will have at least two principal components:

- the channel (distribution channel);
- consumers (purchasers/final users).

Be sure to draw a total market map rather than just the part you currently deal with. The purpose of this is to ensure that you understand your market dynamics properly. For example beware of writing in only the word 'Distributor' if there are, in fact, different kinds of distributors that behave in different ways and that supply different customers. This is explained in more detail below under the heading, 'Leverage points'.

With quantification playing an important part later on in the process, it is useful to mark along each 'route' the volumes and/or values which go down that route (guestimate if necessary). Also, note your market share, if known, as illustrated in Figure 4.3.

Along the market map, ensure you include all the stages that play a part in the flow of products between suppliers and final users.

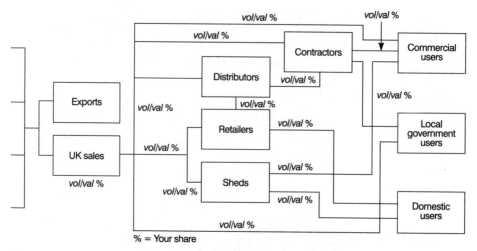

Figure 4.3 Market map with volumes and/or values on each route

These stages will, therefore, include points at which a transaction takes place
and/or where influence/advice/decisions occur (not necessarily a transaction)
about which products to use. These influencers should also appear on the
market map, as shown in Figure 4.4, just as if they were a transaction stage.

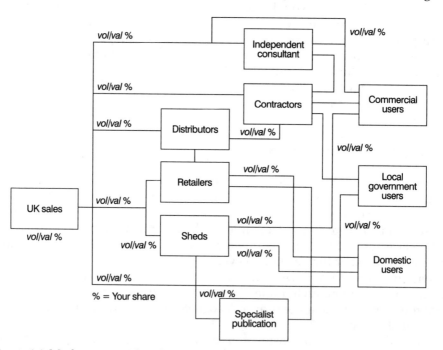

Figure 4.4 Market map with influencers

These transaction stages are referred to as 'junctions', with each junction on a market map positioned hierarchically, according to how close it is to the final user. The last junction along the market map would, therefore, be the final user. The stages in the purchasing procedure found in business-to-business markets are regarded as a single junction (hence their enclosure in one box on the earlier example of a market map).

For most market maps, the decision on which junction a particular activity should be placed will be very clear. However, there will be instances where the decision is not immediately apparent. For example a co-operative may simply replace a retail outlet or a wholesaler, in which case it could just as easily be placed in the same junction as the retailer or wholesaler, as appropriate. Alternatively, a co-operative may source its products from either a wholesaler, or direct from the manufacturer – here, it is clear to position the co-operative on the market map at a stage which is nearest to the final user. Following the same guidelines, the consultant would be placed in a junction one stage below the membership.

Note at each junction, if applicable, all the currently understood different types of companies/customers which occur there, along with the number as suggested in Figure 4.5.

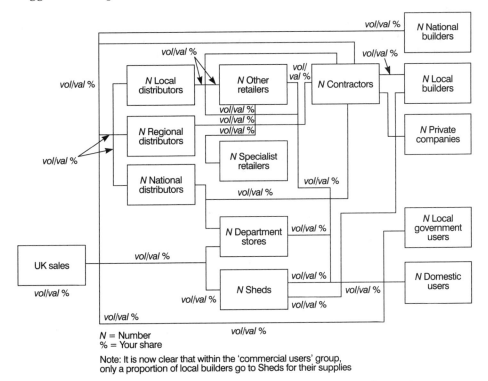

Figure 4.5 Market map with different company/customer types, their volumes and/or values, number of each type and your market share

Allocate to these different company/customer types the volumes and/or values they deal with (guestimate if necessary). Also, note your market share, if known.

The market mapping routine may already be challenging the traditional lists of company/customer types at the various junctions around which you currently conduct your marketing effort. In such instances replace what now appears to be the out-of-date list with the new list. The segmentation process you are now progressing through does, however, test the validity of your list during later steps.

Leverage points

Now, note those junctions where decisions are made about which of the competing products/services should be purchased by outlining them in **bold**. Attach to each type the approximate number of business units/individual purchasers found in it. Clearly, in those instances where one type has been split into two in order to distinguish between a leverage point and a non-leverage point, for example CB1 and CB2, only a total number for the CB type as a whole can be entered.

The inclusion of leverage points is illustrated in Figure 4.6.

So far, we have mapped out the different transactions that take place in your market all the way through to the final user, and seen how the transactions

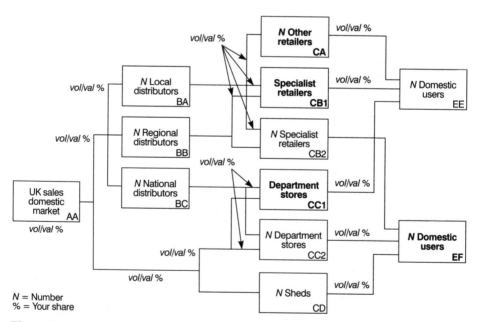

Figure 4.6 Leverage points on a market map for two junctions

relate to each other. By quantifying these various 'routes' and determining your company's share along them, we have identified the most important routes and seen your company's position along each of them.

By then looking at where decisions are made between the producers/ services of competing suppliers, we have identified a number of stages (junctions) where segmentation could occur. For most companies, it is recommended that segmentation should first take place at the junction furthest away from the supplier/manufacturer, where decisions are made.

Most importantly, however, is the fact that we now have a clearer understanding of the structure of our market and how it works.

Who buys and what they buy

A useful method for dealing with this stage of market segmentation is to refer to the market map and, at each point at which there is a critical purchase influence, attempt to describe the characteristics of the customers who belong to it. The descriptions can consist of a single characteristic, or a combination, whichever is appropriate to the market being looked at.

This is when analysis of customer attributes becomes important. It seeks to find some way of describing the customer groups located in our previous analysis for the purpose of communicating with them. For clearly, however clever we might be in isolating segments, unless we can find some way of describing them so that we can address them through our communication programme, our efforts will have been to no avail.

Demographic descriptors have been found to be the most useful method for this purpose. For consumer markets, this is age, sex, education, stage in the family life cycle, and socio-economic groupings. This kind of information is readily available from census data in most of the advanced economies. This latter method describes people by their social status in life as represented by their jobs. Not surprisingly, some categories, for example those that include most of the professions and senior managers, are light television viewers; consequently, if they are your target market, it does not make much sense to advertise your product or service on television. However, they can be effectively reached by means of certain newspapers and magazines, where they comprise the principal readership.

From this, it will be gathered that there is a very useful correlation between readership and viewing patterns and these socio-economic groupings, and this can be most useful in helping us to communicate cost-effectively with our target market by means of advertising. Obviously, however, if we have no real idea of who our target market is, then we are unlikely to be able to take advantage of this convenient method.

It is obvious that, at different stages in the family cycle, we have different needs, and this can be another useful way of describing our market. Banks and insurance companies have been particularly adept at developing products especially for certain age categories. In this respect, because of the gradually reducing relevance of socio-economic group as a predictor of behaviour, there is an emerging concept of 'contexts', such as 'wellness', 'awareness', 'Euroness', 'traditionalism', 'expectism' and 'homecentredness', each one being related to life stages such as 'singles', 'nesters', 'developers' and 'elders'. Thus, Laura Ashley would clearly be in the 'traditionalism' context, while The Body Shop would probably be in the 'wellness' context.

Additionally, a number of geodemographic databases, such as the UK's ACORN (A Classification of Regional Neighbourhood Groups), which classifies all households according to 38 different neighbourhood types and is also based on census data, is particularly useful for the retailing business because, when used in conjunction with market research, it can accurately predict consumption patterns in specific geographical locations.

For industrial markets, SIC (Standard Industrial Classification) categories, number of employees, turnover and production processes have been found to be useful demographic descriptors.

What is bought

In respect of what is bought, the value of the market map should now become apparent. We are really talking about the actual structure of markets in the form of volume, value, the physical characteristics of products, place of purchase, frequency of purchase, price paid, and so on. This tells us, firstly if there are any groups of products (or outlets, or price categories, etc.) which are growing static, or declining, i.e. where the opportunities are and where the problems are.

However, apart from telling us how our market works, it also gives us a good understanding of the market structure.

The next task is to list all relevant competitive products/services, whether or not you manufacture them, ensuring to unbundle all the components of a purchase so that you arrive at a comprehensive list of 'what is bought'.

Features to take into account when drawing up your list include:

- Type of product – e.g. cleaners, galvanizers, installed, flat pack, made up, resident engineers, on-call engineers, bundled with a service package, etc.
- Specification – 100 per cent purity, 98 per cent purity, tolerance levels, percentage failure rate, etc.
- Colour – red, white, blue, pastel, garish, etc.
- Size of package – single, multiple family pack, 5 litre, 20 kg, bulk, etc.
- Volume used – small, medium, large, very large, etc.
- Level/intensity of use – high, medium, low, etc.
- Type of service – testing service, technical advice (which is sometimes, unintentionally, provided by the sales force), evaluation analysis.
- End-use application – where a single final user department or individual utilizes your product/service for a number of different end-use applications, these should be listed here. For example the office services department may require cleaning

services, but the cleaning requirements of the public areas, general office areas and the manufacturing plan (particularly if the manufacturing process involves precision instruments) could all be different. Another example has been identified in the domestic paint market, where the selection process for paint differs according to the type of room it is being bought for – the buying criteria for gloss in the lounge being different from the buying criteria for gloss in the bedroom.

- Brand – manufacturer's, own label, single brand only, any major brand, only local brands, high profile brands.
- Country of origin – UK, German, French, Scandinavian, Western European, Eastern European, Japanese, etc.
- Independent influencers, advisers, consultants (complementing or competing with the technical/advisory services provided by the manufacturers/suppliers) – specialist publications, consumer publications, accountants, financial advisers, consultants, etc. if they appear at junctions used by buyers at the junction being segmented.
- Type of delivery – next day (or a listing of the competing products which provide this, e.g. courier, first class), within four hours, collected, automatically triggered via links with inventory control systems, etc.
- Volume of purchase – large, medium, low (or by a more precise breakdown if appropriate).
- Value of purchase – high, medium, low (or by a more precise breakdown if appropriate).
- Range of products – all, single, across the range, those at the top/middle/bottom of the range, etc.

The resulting list could be as follows:

- Lawnmowers – hover, cylinder, rotary, petrol driven, manual, electrically driven, 12" cut, 16" cut, any mower with a branded engine, extended warranty, with after-sales service, etc.
- Paints – emulsion, gloss, non-drip coat, 5 litre cans, 2 litre cans, environmentally friendly, bulk, etc.
- Petrol stations – self-service, forecourt service, with loyalty programme, etc.

As part of this step, and without attempting at this stage to link this step with the earlier step, list all the channels (if appropriate) where the listed range of products/services is bought. Note that this only refers to the products/services supplied/manufactured by you and your competitors: it therefore excludes the sourcing details for independent influencers, advisors, consultants, etc.

The channel list could include direct/mail order, distributor, department store, national chain, regional chain, local independent retailer, tied retailer, supermarket, wholesalers, shed, specialist supplier, street stall, through a buying group, through a buying club, door-to-door, local/high street/out-of-town shop, etc.

Also, draw up a list which covers the different frequencies of purchase experienced for your own, and your competitors' products/services.

The purchase frequency list could include daily, weekly, monthly, seasonally, every two years, at 50 000 miles, occasionally, as needs, only in emergencies, degrees of urgency, infrequency, rarely, special event, only during sales, at the bottom of the market, etc.

Next, draw up a further separate list covering the different methods of purchase and, if applicable, the different purchasing organizations and procedures observed in your market.

Examples that may help in drawing up your list include:

● Methods of purchase – credit card, charge card, cash, direct debit, standing order, credit terms, Switch, outright purchase, lease-hire, lease-purchase, negotiated price, sealed bid, etc.
● Purchasing organization – centralized or decentralized; structure and distribution of power in the decision-making unit (DMU), which could be as equally applicable in a household as in a business, e.g. decision to purchase made at one level, with the choice of suitable suppliers able to meet the specification, price, etc. made at a technical level, negotiating of price left to the purchasing department and the final decision left to senior management.

Who buys what

Next, attempt to identify for each active 'who', all the unique combinations of 'what is bought' observed on their particular buying activity. The resulting cascade produces a large number of micro segments, each of which should have a volume or value figure attached. These can be reduced in number by determining the important from the unimportant and by removing anything that is obviously superfluous.

Some preliminary screening at this stage is vital in order to cut this long list down to manageable proportions. This will also act as a preliminary form of market segmentation.

Why they buy

The second part of analysing customer behaviour is trying to understand why customers behave the way they do, for, surely, if we can explain the behaviour of our customers, we are in a better position to sell to them.

Basically, there are two principal theories of customer behaviour. One theory refers to the rational customer, who seeks to maximize satisfaction or utility. This customer's behaviour is determined by the utility derived from a purchase at the margin compared with the financial outlay and other opportunities foregone. While such a view of customers provides some important insights into behaviour, it must be remembered that many markets do not work this way at all, there being many examples of a growth in demand with every rise in price.

Another view of customer behaviour that helps to explain this phenomenon is that which describes the psycho-socio customer, whose attitudes and behaviour are affected by family, work, prevailing cultural patterns, reference groups, perceptions, aspirations, and life style.

While such theories also provide useful insights, they rarely explain the totality of customer behaviour. For example it is interesting to know that opinion leaders are often the first to adopt new ideas and new products, but unless these people can be successfully identified and communicated with, this information is of little practical use to us.

The most useful and practical way of explaining customer behaviour has been found to be benefit segmentation, i.e. the benefits sought by customers when they buy a product. For example some customers buy products for their functional characteristics (product), for economy (price), for convenience and availability (place), for emotional reasons (promotion), or for a combination of the reasons (a trade off). Otherwise, how else can the success of firms such as Rolls-Royce, Harrods, and many others be explained? Understanding the benefits sought by customers helps us to organize our marketing mix in the way most likely to appeal to our target market.

Bringing it all together

Our segmentation is now almost complete. The third step involves taking each significant cluster identified earlier (of who buys and what they buy) and listing why they buy. In other words, what benefits are they seeking by buying what they buy?

The final step is to look for clusters of segments that share the same, or similar, needs and to apply to the resulting clusters the organization's minimum volume/value criteria to determine their viability.* While this final step can be difficult and time-consuming, any care lavished on this part of the market segmentation process will pay handsome dividends at later stages of the planning process.

Table 4.1 provides a summary of bases for market segmentation.

Perhaps the best known example of this process is the toothpaste market, shown in Table 4.2.

---

* A computer program, called 'Market Segment Master' is available for this task. For details, write to Professor Malcolm McDonald, Cranfield School of Management, Cranfield, Bedford, England MK43 OAL.

Table 4.1 Summary of bases for market segmentation

What is bought	Price
	Outlets
	Physical characteristics
	Geography
	Applications
Who buys	Demographic
	Socio-economic
	Brand loyalty
	Heavy/light users
	Personality, traits, life styles
Why	Benefits
	Attitudes
	Perceptions
	Preferences

Table 4.2 Segmentation of the toothpaste market

	Worrier	*Sociable*	*Sensory*	*Independent*
Who buys				
Socio-economic	CI C2	B CI C2	CI C2 D	A B
Demographics	Large families 25–40 Conservative: hypochondriosis	Teens Young smokers High sociability: active	Children High self involvement: hedonists	Males 35–50 High autonomy Value oriented
What is bought				
% of total market	50%	30%	15%	5%
Product examples	Crest	McLeans; Ultra Bright	Colgate (stripe)	Own label
Product physics	Large canisters	Large tubes	Medium tubes	Small tubes
Price paid	Low	High	Medium	Low
Outlet	Supermarket	Supermarket	Supermarket	Independent
Purchase frequency	Weekly	Monthly	Monthly	Quarterly
Why				
Benefits sought	Stop decay	Attract attention	Flavour	Price
Potential for growth	Nil	High	Medium	Nil

Adapted from R. Haley, 'Benefit Segmentation: a decision-oriented research tool', *Journal of Marketing*, Vol. 32, July 1968.

Why market segmentation is vital in planning

In today's highly competitive world, few companies can afford to compete only on price, for the product has not yet been sold that someone, somewhere, cannot sell cheaper – apart from which, in many markets it is rarely the cheapest product that succeeds anyway.

What this means is that we have to find some way of differentiating ourselves from the competition and the answer lies in market segmentation.

The truth is that very few companies can afford to be 'all things to all people'. The main aim of market segmentation as part of the planning process is to enable a firm to target its effort on the most promising opportunities. But what is an opportunity for firm A is not necessarily an opportunity for firm B. So a firm needs to develop a typology of the customer or segment it prefers, for this can be an instrument of great productivity in the marketplace.

The whole point of segmentation is that a company must either:

- Define its markets broadly enough to ensure that its costs for key activities are competitive; or
- Define its markets in such a way that it can develop specialised skills in serving them to overcome a relative cost disadvantage.

Both have to be related to a firm's distinctive competence and to that of its competitors.

All of this should come to the fore as a result of the marketing audit referred to in Chapter 3 and should be summarized in the SWOT analyses. In particular, the differential benefits of a firm's product or service should be beyond doubt to all key members of the company.

Correct market definition is crucial for:

- share measurement;
- growth measurement;
- specification of target customers;
- recognition of relevant competitors;
- formulation of marketing objectives and strategies.

To summarize, the objectives of market segmentation are:

- To help determine marketing direction through the analysis and understanding of trends and buyer behaviour.
- To help determine realistic and obtainable marketing and sales objectives.
- To help improve decision making by forcing managers to consider in depth the options ahead.

Why market segmentation is important in key account planning

A deep understanding of their market, how it works, how it breaks down into natural segments and the specific nature of the unique value sought by each of these segments, will obviously give key account managers a significant advantage in building long-term relationships with their customers.

Selecting and targeting market segments

The methodology described here should be read carefully by key account managers, because exactly the same methodology (but using different variables), will be used for identifying and targeting key accounts.

We have seen that a business should define its markets in such a way that it can ensure that its costs for key activities will be competitive. Or, it should define the markets it serves in such a way that it can develop specialized skills in servicing those markets and hence overcome a relative cost disadvantage. Both, of course, have to be related to a company's distinctive competence.

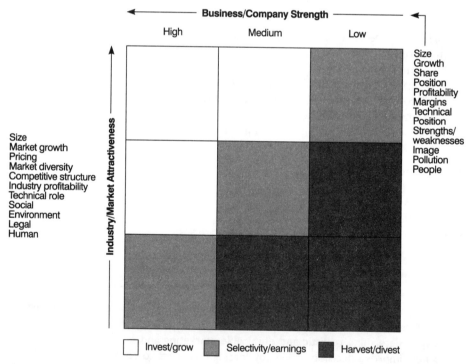

Figure 4.7 A nine-box directional policy matrix

However, the approach developed in the late 1960s by the Boston Consulting Group is fairly criticized for relying on two single factors, i.e. relative market share and market growth, neither of which explain business success on their own. To overcome this difficulty, and to provide a more flexible approach, General Electric and McKinsey jointly developed a multi-factor approach using the same fundamental ideas as the Boston Consulting Group. They used *industry attractiveness* and *business strengths* as the two main axes and built up these dimensions from a number of variables. Using these variables, and some scheme for weighting them according to their importance, products (or businesses) are classified into one of nine cells in a 3 × 3 matrix. Thus, the same purpose is served as in the Boston matrix (i.e. comparing investment opportunities among products or businesses) but with the difference that multiple criteria are used. These criteria vary according to circumstances, but often include those shown in Figure 4.7.

It is not necessary, however, to use a nine-box matrix, and many managers prefer to use a four-box matrix similar to the Boston box. Indeed this is the authors' preferred methodology, as it seems to be more easily understood by, and useful to, practising managers.

The four-box directional policy matrix (DPM) is shown in Figure 4.8. Here, the circles represent sales into an industry, market or segment and in the same way as in the Boston matrix, each is proportional to that segment's contribution to turnover.

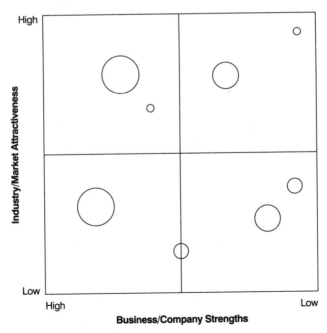

Figure 4.8 A four-box directional policy matrix

The difference in this case is that, rather than using only two variables, the criteria which are used for each axis are totally relevant and specific to each company using the matrix. It shows:

● Markets categorized on a scale of attractiveness to the firm.
● The firm's relative strengths in each of these markets.
● The relative importance of each market.

The specific criteria to be used should be decided by key executives using the device, but a generalized list for the vertical axis is given in Table 4.3. It is

Table 4.3 Factors contributing to market attractiveness

Market factors
Size (money units or both)
Size of key segments
Growth rate per year: total segments
Diversity of market
Sensitivity to price, service features and external factors
Cyclicality
Seasonality
Bargaining power of upstream suppliers
Bargaining power of downstream suppliers

Financial and economic factors
Contribution margins
Leveraging factors, such as economies of scale and experience
Barriers to entry or exit (both financial and non-financial)
Capacity utilization

Technological factors
Maturity and volatility
Complexity
Differentiation
Patents and copyrights
Manufacturing process technology required

Competition
Types of competitors
Degree of concentration
Changes in type and mix
Entries and exits
Changes in share
Substitution by new technology
Degrees and types of integration

Socio-political factors in your environment
Social attitudes and trends
Laws and government agency regulations
Influence with pressure groups and government representatives
Human factors, such as unionization and community acceptance

advisable to use no more than five or six factors, otherwise the exercise becomes too complex and loses its focus. Read on, however, before selecting these factors, as essential methodological instructions on the construction of a portfolio matrix follow.

Preparation for constructing the matrix

Prior to commencing analysis, the following preparation is recommended:

i) Product profiles should be available for all products/services to be scored.
ii) The markets in which the products/services compete should be clearly defined.
iii) Define the time period being scored. Three years are recommended.
iv) Define the competitors against which the products/services will be scored.
v) Ensure sufficient data is available to score the factors (where no data is available, this is no problem as long as a sensible approximation can be made for the factors).
vi) Ensure up-to-date sales forecasts are available for all products/services, plus any new products/services.

Analysis team

In order to improve the quality of scoring, it is recommended that a group of people from a number of different functions score, as this encourages the challenging of traditional views through discussion. It is recommended that there should be no more than six people involved in the analysis.

Ten steps to producing the DPM

Step 1   Should define the products/services (segments) for markets that are to be used during the analysis.
Step 2   Should define the criteria for market attractiveness.
Step 3   Should score the relevant segments.
Step 4   Should define the organization's relative strengths for each segment.
Step 5   Should analyse and draw conclusions from the relative position of each segment.
Step 6   Should draw conclusions from the analysis with a view to generating objectives and strategies.
Step 7   (Optional) Should position the circles on the box assuming no change to current policies. That is to say, a forecast should be made of the future position of the circles.

Step 8   Should redraw the portfolio to position the circles where the organization wants them to be. That is to say, the objectives they wish to achieve for each segment.

Step 9   Should detail the strategies to be implemented to achieve the objectives.

Step 10   Should detail the appropriate financial consequences in terms of growth rate by segment and return on sales.

Two key definitions

Market attractiveness is a measure of the potential of the marketplace to yield growth in sales and profits. It is important to stress that this should be an objective assessment of market attractiveness using data external to the organization. The criteria themselves will, of course, be determined by the organization carrying out the exercise and will be relevant to the objectives the organization is trying to achieve, but it should be independent of the organization's position in its markets.

Business strengths/position is a measure of an organization's actual strengths in the marketplace (i.e. the degree to which it can take advantage of a market opportunity). Thus, it is an objective assessment of an organization's ability to satisfy market needs relative to competitors.

The process

Step 1   List the population of products/services for markets that you intend to include in the matrix.

The list can consist of countries, companies, subsidiaries, regions, products, markets, segments, customers, distributors, or any other unit of analysis that is important.

The DPM can be used at any level in an organization and for any kind of business unit.

For the purpose of this chapter, we will assume the matrix contains segments.

Step 2   Define market attractiveness factors.

In this step, you should list the factors you wish to consider in comparing the attractiveness of your segments.

It is also important to list the segments that you intend to apply the criteria to before deciding on the criteria themselves, since the purpose of the vertical axis is to discriminate between more and less attractive segments. The criteria themselves must be specific to the population and must not be changed for different segments in the same population.

This is explained in the following simple example.

Factors	Example weight
Growth rate	40
Accessible market size	20
Profit potential	40
Total	**100**

Note: As profit = market size × margin × growth, it would be reasonable to expect a weighting against each of these to be at least as shown, although an even higher weight on growth would be understandable in some circumstances (in which case, the corresponding weight for the others should be reduced).

This is a combination of a number of factors. These factors, however, can usually be summarized under three headings.

1 Growth rate – Average annual growth rate of revenue spent by that segment (percentage growth 1994 over 1993, plus percentage growth 1995 over 1994, plus percentage growth 1996 over 1995, divided by 3). If preferred, compound average growth rate could be used.

2 Accessible market size – An attractive market is not only large – it can also be accessed. One way of calculating this is to estimate the total revenue of the segment in t + 3 (a forecast for three years from the current year), less revenue impossible to access, regardless of investment made. Alternatively, total market size can be used, which is the most frequent method, as it does not involve any managerial judgement to be made that could distort the truth. This latter method is the preferred method. A market size factors score is simply the score multiplied by the weight (20 as in the previous example).

3 Profit potential – This is much more difficult to deal with and will vary considerably, according to industry. For example Porter's five forces model could be used to estimate the profit potential of a segment, as in the following example:

Sub-factors	10 = Low × Weight 0 = High	Weighted factor score
1 Intensity of competition	50	
2 Threat of substitute	5	
3 Threat of new entrants	5	
4 Power of suppliers	10	
5 Power of customer	30	
Profit potential factor score		

Alternatively, a combination of these and industry-specific factors could be used. In the case of the pharmaceutical industry, for example the factors could be:

Sub-factors	High Medium Low × Weight	Weighted factor score
Unmet medical needs (efficacy)	30	
Unmet medical needs (safety)	25	
Unmet medical needs (convenience)	15	
Price potential	10	
Competitive intensity	10	
Cost of market entry	10	
Profit potential factor score		

These are clearly a proxy for profit potential. Each is weighted according to its importance. The weights add up to 100 in order to give a profit potential factor score, as in the Porter's five forces example above.

Note that, following this calculation, the profit potential factor score is simply multiplied by the weight (40 as in the previous example).

Variations – Naturally, growth, size and profit will not encapsulate the requirements of all organizations. For example in the case of an orchestra, artistic satisfaction may be an important consideration. In another case, social considerations could be important. In yet another, cyclicality may be a factor. It is possible, then, to add another heading, such as 'Risk' or 'Other' to the three factors listed at the beginning of Step 2. In general, however, it should be possible to reduce it to just the three main ones, with sub-factors incorporated into these, as shown.

Step 3   Score the relevant segments.

In this step the segments should be scored against the criteria defined in Step 1.

Can market attractiveness factors change while constructing the DPM? The answer to this is no. Once agreed, under no circumstances should market attractiveness factors be changed, otherwise the attractiveness of markets is not being evaluated against common criteria and the matrix becomes meaningless. Scores, however, will be specific to each market.

Can the circles move vertically? No is the obvious answer, although yes is also possible, providing the matrix shows the current level of attractiveness at the present time. This implies carrying out one set of calculations for the present time according to market attractiveness factors, in order to locate markets on the vertical axis, then carrying out another set of calculations for a future period (say, in three years' time), based on our forecasts according to the same factors. In practice, it is easier to carry out only the latter calculation, in which case the circles can only move horizontally.

Step 4   Define business strengths/position.

   1 This is a measure of an organization's actual strengths in the marketplace and will differ by segment.
      These factors will usually be a combination of an organization's relative strengths versus competitors in connection with customer-facing needs, i.e. those things that are required by the customer.
      These can often be summarized under:

   ● Product requirements;
   ● Price requirements;
   ● Service requirements;
   ● Promotion requirements.

   The weightings given to each should be specific to each segment. In the same way that 'profit' on the market attractiveness axis can be broken down into sub-headings, so can each of the above be broken down further and analysed. Indeed, this is strongly recommended. These sub-factors should be dealt with in the same way as the sub-factors described under 'market attractiveness'. For example in the case of pharmaceuticals, product strengths could be represented by:

   ● Relative product strengths;
   ● Relative product safety;
   ● Relative product convenience;
   ● Relative cost effectiveness.

   2 Broadening the analysis.
      It will be clear that an organization's relative strengths in meeting customer-facing needs will be a function of its capabilities in connection with industry-wide success factors. For example if a depot is necessary in each major town/city for any organization to succeed in an industry and the organization carrying out the analysis doesn't have this, then it is likely that this will account for its poor performance under 'customer service', which is, of course, a customer requirement. Likewise, if it is

necessary to have low feedstock costs for any organization to succeed in an industry and the organization carrying out the analysis doesn't have this, then it is likely that this will account for its poor performance under 'price', which is, of course, a customer requirement.

Thus, in the same way that sub-factors should be estimated in order to arrive at 'market attractiveness' factors, so an assessment of an organization's capabilities in respect of industry-wide success factors could be made in order to understand what needs to be done in the organization in order to satisfy customer needs better. This assessment, however, is quite separate from the quantification of the business strengths/position axis and its purpose is to translate the analysis into actionable propositions for other functions within the organization, such as purchasing, production, distribution, and so on.

3 How to deal with business strengths/position.

The first of these concerns the quantification of business strengths within a segment. Many books for the manager are not particularly useful when used to construct a marketing plan. Few of the factors they mention take account of the need for a company to make an 'offer' to a particular segment that has a sustainable competitive advantage over the 'offers' of relevant competitors.

The only way a company can do this is to understand the real needs and wants of the chosen customer group, find out by means of market research how well these needs are being met by the products on offer, and then seek to satisfy these needs better than their competitors.

The following is a typical calculation to assess the strength of a company in a market. The information has been gathered by means of a self-assessment questionnaire, where the following three questions are used to plot the organization's position on the horizontal axis (competitive position/business strengths):

(i)   What are the few key things that any competitor has to do right to succeed (i.e. what are the critical success factors, also known as CSFs in this segment).

(ii) How important is each of these critical success factors (measured comparatively using a score out of 100)?

(iii) How do you and each of your competitors score (out of 10) on each of the critical success factors?

These questions yield the information necessary to make an overall assessment of an organization's competitive strengths:

Critical success factors (What are the few key things that any competition has to do right to succeed?)	Weighting (How important is each of these CSFs? Score out of 100)		Strengths/weaknesses analysis (Score yourself and each of your main competitors out of 10 on each of the CSFs, then multiply the score by the weight)			
				Competition		
			You	Comp A	Comp B	Comp C
1 Product	20		9 = 1.8	6 = 1.2	5 = 1.0	4 = 0.8
2 Price	10		8 = 0.8	5 = 0.5	6 = 0.6	10 = 0.1
3 Service	50		5 = 2.5	9 = 4.5	7 = 3.5	6 = 3.0
4 Image	20		8 = 1.6	8 = 1.6	5 = 1.0	3 = 0.6
These should normally be viewed from the customer's point of view	**Total 100**	**Total score × weight**	**6.7**	**7.8**	**6.1**	**5.4**

From this it will be seen that:

● this organization is not the best;
● all competitors score more than 5.0.

The problem with this and many similar calculations is that rarely will this method discriminate sufficiently well to indicate the relative strengths of a number of products in a particular company's segment portfolio, and many of the organization's segments would appear on the left of the matrix.

Some method is required to prevent all products appearing on the left of the matrix. This can be achieved by using a ratio, as in the Boston matrix. This will indicate a company's position relative to the best in the market.

In the example provided, Competitor A has most strengths in the market, so our organization needs to make some improvements. To reflect this, our weighted score should be compared with that of Competitor A (the highest weighted score). Thus 6.7:7.8 = 0.86:1.

If we were to plot this on a logarithmic scale on the horizontal axis, this would place our organization to the right of the dividing line as follows:

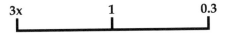

(We should make the left-hand extreme point 3x and start the scale on the right at 0.3.)

A scale of 3x to 0.3 has been chosen because such a band is likely to encapsulate most extremes of competitive advantage. If it doesn't, just change it to suit your own circumstances.

Step 5   Producing the DPM.
Finally, circles should be drawn on a four-box matrix, using segment size (as defined in Step 2 above) to determine the area of the circle. An organization's market share can be put in as a 'cheese' in each circle. Alternatively, an organization's own sales into each segment can be used.

   In practice, however, it is advisable to do both and compare them in order to see how closely actual sales match the opportunities.

Step 6   Analysis and generation of marketing objectives and strategies.
The objective of producing the DPM is to see the portfolio of segments relative to each other in the context of the criteria used. This analysis should indicate whether the portfolio is well balanced or not and should give a clear indication of any problems. As an option, it is sometimes advisable to move to Step 7 at this point.

Step 7   (Optional) Forecasting.
The forecast position of the circles should now be made. This is simply done by re-scoring the segments in three years' time, assuming the organization doesn't change its strategies (see Step 3). This will indicate whether the position is getting worse or better.

   It is not absolutely necessary to change the scores on the vertical axis (see Step 3).

Step 8   Setting marketing objectives.
This involves changing the volumes/values and/or market share (marketing objectives) and the scores on the horizontal axis (relative strength in market) in order to achieve the desired volumes/values. Conceptually, one is picking up the circle and moving/revising it without specifying how this is to be achieved. Strategies are then defined, which involve words and changes to individual CSF scores (Step 9).

Step 9   Spell out strategies.
This involves making specific statements about the marketing strategies to be employed to achieve the desired volumes/values.

Step 10 Sales and profit forecasts.
Once this is done, organizations should be asked to do the following:

1 Plot average percentage growth in sales revenue by segment
(t − 3 to t0).

Plot average percentage ROS by segment (t − 3 to t0).

2 Plot forecast average percentage growth in sales revenue by segment
(t0 to t + 3). This will show clearly whether past performance
and, more importantly, forecasts match the segment rating exercise
above. This should preferably be done by someone else
(e.g. accountants).

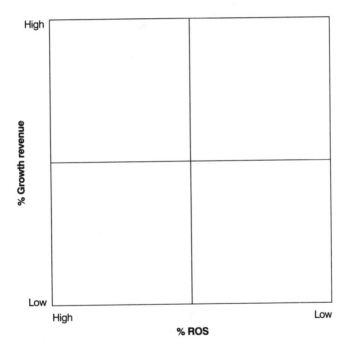

Figure 4.9

An example of a completed matrix is given in Figure 4.10, which shows
a portfolio completed for an agrochemical company. It shows the size
and direction of the company's main segments now and in three years'
time.

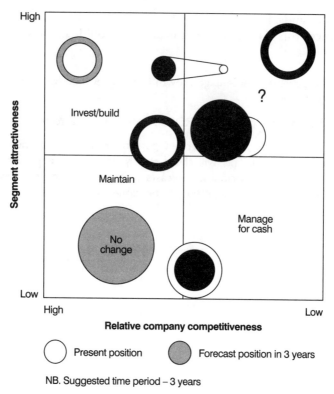

Figure 4.10 Portfolio analysis: directional policy matrix

Setting marketing objectives and strategies

The general marketing directions that lead to the setting of marketing objectives flow, of course, from the portfolio analysis described above and revolve around the following logical decisions:

1 *Maintain.* This usually refers to the 'cash cow' type of product/market and reflects the desire to maintain competitive positions.
2 *Improve.* This usually refers to the 'star' type of products/market and reflects the desire to improve the competitive position in attractive markets.
3 *Harvest.* This usually refers to the 'dog' type of product/market and reflects the desire to relinquish competitive position in favour of short-term profit and cash flow.
4 *Exit.* This also usually refers to the 'dog' type of product/market, also sometimes the 'question mark', and reflects a desire to divest because of a weak competitive position or because the cost of staying in it is prohibitive and the risk associated with improving its position is too high.
5 *Enter.* This usually refers to a new business area.

Table 4.4 Strategies suggested by portfolio matrix analysis

Business strengths

	High	Low
High	Invest for growth Defend leadership, gain if possible Accept moderate short-term profits and negative cash flow Consider geographic expansion, product line expansion, product differentiation Upgrade production Introduction effort Aggressive marketing posture viz. selling, advertising, pricing, sales promotion, service levels, as appropriate	Opportunistic The options are: 1 Move it to the left if resources are available to invest in it 2 Keep a low profile until funds are available 3 Divest to a buyer able to exploit the opportunity

Market attractiveness

		Selective*	Manage for profit
Low	Maintain market position, manage for sustained earnings Maintain market position in most successful product lines Prune less successful product lines Differentiate products to maintain share of key segments Limit discretionary marketing expenditure Stabilize prices, except where a temporary aggressive stance is necessary to maintain market share		Acknowledge low growth Do not view as a 'marketing' problem Identify and exploit growth segments Emphasize product quality to avoid 'commodity' competition Systematically improve productivity Assign talented managers	Prune product line aggressively Maximize cash flow Minimize marketing expenditure Maintain or raise prices at the expense of volume
	3.0	1.0	0.3

* Selective refers to those products or markets which fall on or near the vertical dividing line in a directional policy matrix.

	Invest for growth	Maintain market position, manage for earnings	Selective	Manage for cash	Opportunistic development
Market share	Maintain or increase dominance	Maintain or slightly milk for earnings	Maintain selectivity – segment	Forego share for profit	Invest selectively in share
Products	Differentiation – line expansion	Prune for less successful differentiate for segments	Emphasize product quality	Agressively prune	Differentiation – line expansion
Price	Lead – aggressive pricing for share	Stabilize prices/raise	Maintain or raise	Raise	Aggressive – price for share
Promotion	Aggressive marketing	Limit	Maintain selectively	Minimize	Aggressive marketing
Distribution	Broaden distribution	Hold wide distribution pattern	Segment	Gradually withdraw distribution	Limited coverage
Cost control	Tight control – go for scale economies	Emphasize cost reduction viz variable costs	Tight control	Aggressively reduce fixed & variable	Tight – but not at expense of entrepreneurship
Production	Expand, invest (organic acquisition, joint venture)	Maximize capacity utilization	Increase productivity e.g. specialization	Free up capacity	Invest
R&D	Expand – invest	Focus on specific projects	Invest selectively	None	Invest
Personnel	Upgrade management in key functional areas	Maintain, reward efficiency, tighten organization	Allocate key managers	Cut back organization	Invest
Investment	Fund growth	Limit fixed investment	Invest selectively	Minimize & divest opportunistically	Fund growth
Working capital	Reduce in process – extend credit	Tighten credit – reduce accounts receivable increase inventory turn	Reduce	Agressively reduce	Invest

Figure 4.11 Programme guidelines suggested for different positioning on the directional policy matrix

Great care should be taken, however, not to follow slavishly any set of 'rules' or guidelines related to the above. Also, the use of pejorative labels such as 'dog', 'cash cow', and so on should be avoided if possible.

A full list of marketing guidelines as a precursor to objective setting is given in Table 4.4. Figure 4.11 sets out a fuller list that includes guidelines for functions other than marketing. One word of warning, however. Such general guidelines should not be followed unquestioningly. They are included more as checklists of questions that should be asked about each major product in each major market before setting marketing objectives and strategies.

It is at this stage that the circles in the directional policy matrix can be moved to show their relative size and position in three years' time. You can do this to show, first, where they will be if the company takes no action, and second, where you would ideally prefer them to be. These latter positions will, of course, become the marketing objectives.

Defining and selecting target key accounts

We have seen in some detail the process by which an organization's objectives and strategies can be totally market driven. This is only possible if market segments are first identified and then categorized according to the potential of each for growth in profit over some designated time period and according to the organization's competitive capabilities in meeting customer needs.

Inevitably, this means that there will always be part of our market in the 'low potential/low strengths' box and it is therefore possible that some key accounts within such segments will also fall in this box, as well as in the other three boxes.

Before carrying out the next phase of analysis, it is worth considering this point very seriously, for clearly it will be the key accounts in the 'high potential/high strengths' segments that we should be targeting for our primary growth focus. We should also bear in mind that key accounts in the 'low potential/high strengths' box also need targeting as a major activity in order to protect our current business. Thirdly, we also need to consider key accounts in those segments falling in the 'high potential/low strengths' box, for these are opportunities for future revenue streams. By definition, this means that any key accounts in the 'low potential/low strengths' box should be the last to command our attention, given our scarce resources.

None the less, we still need a methodology for classifying key accounts, irrespective of which box they fall in and this is the purpose of this next section.

Exactly the same steps as those outlined above for classifying segments should be used for key accounts, starting with a full listing of the population of key accounts to be categorized. The Cranfield research showed that the more frequently used criteria for the vertical axis are:

- the available size of spend;
- the margins available;

- the growth rate;
- the location;
- purchasing criteria and processes;
- current suppliers.

Each of these should be quantified, weighted and scored in exactly the same way as for the methodology used in quantifying the vertical axis of the DPM. This way, all key accounts will be spread along the vertical axis, with some above the dividing horizontal line (high potential) and some below (lower potential).

We are now ready to assess our competitive position in each of these key accounts. This chapter contains a detailed explanation of how we can assess our competition position in each account and, once this has been done, a similar methodology can be used to that described in positioning our company along the horizontal axis of the DPM (described earlier in the chapter).

Figure 4.12 shows the resulting matrix, which, not surprisingly, contains exactly the same general advice as for the DPM because the principles are the same.

The team constructing this matrix can use either circles calculated in the same way as for the DPM, or, if they prefer, can just list each key account, perhaps with the available share of spend after each one.

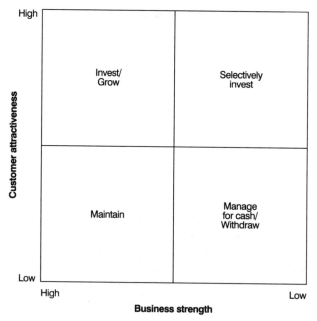

Figure 4.12 Defining and selecting target key accounts

We can now tie this in more closely with the key account categorization given in Chapter 2 (the relational model). This is shown in Figure 4.13.

From this, it will be seen that those relationships classified as Pre-KAM, Early-KAM and Mid-KAM appear on the right of the matrix ('low strengths'), whereas those that have already reached Partnership and Synergistic stages appear on the left. (Please note, it is also possible to have some Mid-KAM accounts on the left.)

Taking each box in turn and starting with the bottom left box ('low potential/ high strengths'), it is possible to work out sensible objectives and strategies for each key account. In this particular box, common sense would dictate retention strategies, as these accounts are likely to continue to deliver excellent revenues for some considerable time, even though some of them may be in static or declining markets. This is especially possible since we already enjoy good relationships with the account and these should be preserved. So, prudence, vigilance and motivation are essential here. More importantly, we should be seeking a good return on our previous investments and any financial investment should mainly be of the maintenance kind. This way, it should be possible to free up cash and resources for investing in key accounts with greater growth potential.

The top left box ('high potential/high strengths') is obviously where we will get much of our growth in sales and profits from. Here, however, a quite aggressive investment approach is justified, providing they are justified by

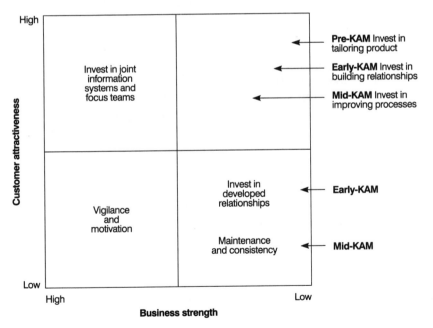

Figure 4.13 Key account strategies

returns. It is probably appropriate to use net present value (NPV) calculations as a basis for evaluating these returns, using a discount rate higher than the cost of capital to reflect the additional risks involved. Any investment here will probably go on developing joint information systems and relationships.

The top right box ('high potential/low strengths') poses a problem, for few organizations have sufficient resources to invest in building better relationships with all accounts falling in this box. Therefore, for each key account, net revenue streams should be forecast for, say, three years, and discounted at the cost of capital (plus a considerable percentage to reflect the high risk involved) in order to evaluate which ones justify investment. Having done this, however, and having selected the ones in which to invest, under no circumstances should financial accounting measures such as NPV be used to control them within the budget year. To do so would be a bit like pulling up a new plant every few weeks to see whether it had grown! Measures such as sales volume, value, 'share of wallet' and the quality of the relationship should be set as objectives. This way, it should be possible to move the selected accounts gradually towards partnership and in some cases towards synergistic relationships, when it will become more appropriate to measure profitability as a control procedure.

Accounts in the final box ('low potential/low strengths') should not occupy too much of our time. Some can be handed over to distributors, while some can be handled by our own personnel, providing all transactions are profitable and deliver net free cash flow.

It will by now be obvious that all other company functions and activities should be consistent with the goals set for key accounts according to the above general categorization. For example some key account managers will be extremely good at managing accounts in the Pre-, Early- and Mid-KAM stages, where selling and negotiating skills are paramount, whereas others will be better suited to managing the more complex business and managerial issues surrounding partnership and synergistic relationships.

To summarize, the effective allocation of an organization's scarce resources, particularly in mature and highly competitive industries, is a major problem for directors and senior managers. Thus, some method has to be found for ensuring current growth in sales and profits, at the same time as investing for future earnings. The methodology outlined in this chapter is a sound way of managing these complex issues.

In the next chapter, we explain how to set objectives and strategies for each key account and how to prepare a strategic plan for each one.

Chapter 5

Key account planning

Introduction

We saw in Chapter 3 the relationship between a strategic plan for a key account and plans for segments, markets and businesses. This was summarized diagrammatically, shown here as Figure 5.1.

We also saw in Chapter 4 the basis on which key accounts should be selected and targeted and how to set appropriate objectives for them over a planning period of about three years. This was also summarized diagrammatically, shown here as Figure 5.2.

The purpose of this chapter is to provide a set of specific and detailed procedures for producing a strategic marketing plan for each key account selected as being worthy of focused attention by the key account team.

An overview of the total process, which we have called the business partnership process is shown as Figure 5.3.

From this, it will be seen that steps 1, 2 and 3 were dealt with in some detail in Chapter 4. It is worth noting again that Porter's five forces analysis of particular industries is probably best done by someone in central support services, as there is clearly little point in a number of key account managers all doing exactly the same analysis. If for some reason this is not practicable, then the job will have to be done by individual key account managers for their own industrial sectors. This, of course, is a prerequisite to the individual account analysis that will be explained in this chapter, as it provides key account managers with a deep analysis of their clients' industry and how it works. It is also worth stressing that steps 4 to 9 are all concerned with the analysis/diagnosis stage that must be completed prior to preparing the strategic plan for each key account. In this respect, steps 4 to 9 are a little like the marketing audit described in detail in Chapter 3.

Corporate plan					
Marketing plan					
Segment plan		Segment plan		Segment plan	
Account plan 1	Account plan 2	Account plan 3	Account plan 4	Account plan 5	Account plan 6

Figure 5.1 The planning hierarchy

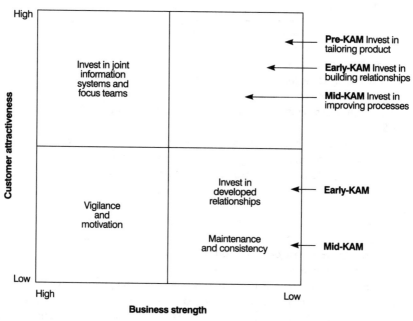

Figure 5.2 Key account strategies

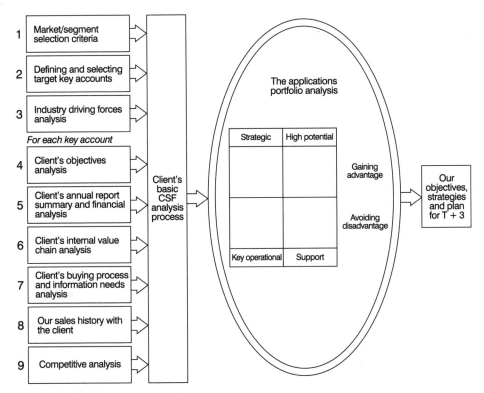

Figure 5.3 Business partnership process

Step 4 Client's objectives analysis

Figure 5.4 should be completed for each key account being targeted. It can be seen that the intention is to take the industry driving forces analysis and apply it specifically to an individual account in order to understand better what advantages and disadvantages it has. The main reason for doing this is to help us to understand ways in which our products or services may enable the client to exploit advantages and minimize disadvantages.

It is not the intention to complete this document as if it were a pro forma. Each heading is intended merely to act as a trigger for some powerful conclusions about your client's competitive situation. This information will be used along with the further information to be gathered in steps 5 to 9.

Client Name	**Industry Driving Forces** (key success factors) What makes the difference between success and failure in this business?	**Situation Analysis** For those factors which make a difference, where does my customer stand?

Strengths Weaknesses | Market: Opportunities Threats

Competitive Advantage
Do my customers or their competitors have any unique competitive advantage?

Present: Advantage Disadvantage	Potential: Advantage Disadvantage

Objective
How can my customers most effectively employ the advantages they have, counter those of their competitors and develop or acquire future competitive advantage?

Exploit current advantage, minimize disadvantage	Develop future advantage, counter potential disadvantage

Figure 5.4 Objectives analysis exercise (industry driving forces)

Step 5 Client's annual report summary and financial analysis

Figure 5.5 enables a summary to be made of a careful reading and analysis of a client's published annual report. Even if there is not a formal report published for the shareholders (say, for example if your client is a subsidiary or division of a larger company), the directors do none the less tend to produce internal reports and newsletters.

1 Major achievements	
2 Major problems/issues	
3 Objectives	
4 Strategies	
5 Conclusions/opportunities	

Figure 5.5 Annual report summary

Financial ratio indicator	Formula	Source					Com-pany stand-ing	Indus-try stand-ing	Does it appear as though improve-ment is needed?		
		Annual report							Yes	No	
Current ratio	$\dfrac{\text{Current assets}}{\text{Current liabilities}}$										
Net profit margin	$\dfrac{\text{Net profit}}{\text{Net sales}}$										
Return on assets	$\dfrac{\text{Net profit}}{\text{Total assets}}$										
Collection period	$\dfrac{\text{Debtors less bad debts}}{\text{Average day's sales}}$										
Stock turnover	$\dfrac{\text{Cost of goods sold}}{\text{Stock}}$										

Description of indicators	**Current ratio**	Measures the liquidity of a company – does it have enough money to pay the bill?
	Net profit margin	Measures the overall profitability of a company by showing the percentage of sales retained as profit after taxes have been paid. If this ratio is acceptable, there probably is no need to calculate the gross profit or operating profit margins
	Return on assets	Evaluates how effectively a company is managed by comparing the profitability of a company and its investments
	Collection period	Measures the activity of debtors. Prolonged collection period means that a company's funds are financing customers and not contributing to cash flow of the company
	Stock turnover	Evaluates how fast funds are flowing through cost of goods sold to produce profit. If stock turns over faster, it is not in the plant as long before it is saleable as a product

Figure 5.6 Financial analysis

Such documents can be a major source of information on what your client believes to be the major issues facing them and their achievements and objectives and strategies – in other words, their hopes for the future.

It is always possible to extract valuable information that can be used in helping you to understand how your organization might be of assistance. This information can now be put alongside the information gleaned from the previous summary.

Figure 5.6 focuses on the financial affairs of your client and concerns information that can also be obtained from annual reports and other published sources. At first sight, this might appear to be some way removed from the reality of selling goods and services to a major account. A little thought, however, will reveal that most organizations today are acutely aware of their:

- current ratios;
- net profit margins;
- return on assets;
- debtor control;
- asset turnover.

The purpose of the analysis contained in Figure 5.6 is to make you acutely aware of the financial issues faced by your client and to encourage you to explore whether any of your products and services could improve any of these ratios. It will be obvious that any supplier who has taken the trouble to work out what impact its products and services have on the customer's bottom line will be preferred to a potential supplier who focuses only on features.

Step 6 Client's internal value chain analysis

Figure 5.7 illustrates an organization's internal value chain, popularized by Professor Michael Porter in his 1982 book on competitive strategies. It is assumed that readers are familiar with this concept. It is introduced here as an invaluable tool for understanding how a major account actually functions. The bottom level shows bought-in goods or services entering the organization, passing through operations, then out to their markets through distribution, marketing and sales and service. Sitting above these core processes are organizational support activities such as human resource management, procurement, and so on.

Investigating how a major account actually manages these core activities can be a substantial task for a key account team, involving, as it does, a deep understanding of the detailed processes of the customer. This could include for example understanding what happens to your goods when they are delivered, where they are stored, how they are handled, how they are moved, how they

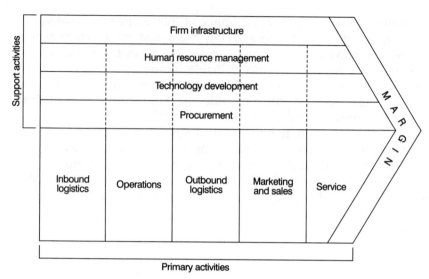

Figure 5.7 The value chain

are unpacked, how they are used, and so on. The purpose of such detailed analysis is to explore what issues and problems are faced by your customer with a view to making improvements.

Figure 5.8 is a very simple illustration of some of these issues and how they could be improved.

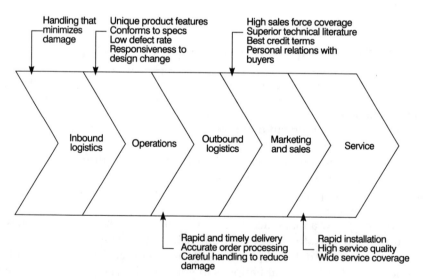

Figure 5.8 Sources of differentiation in the value chain

All information emanating from this analysis can be usefully summarized using a format similar to that shown in Figure 5.9. From this, it will be seen that there are four general headings of customer benefits:

- possibilities for increased revenue for the customer;
- possibilities for cost displacement;
- possibilities for cost avoidance;
- intangible benefits.

Tangible benefits	Product solution	Analysis and comment
Increased revenue		
Increased sales volume		
Enhanced product line		
Cost displacement		
Reduced labour costs		
Reduced equipment costs		
Reduced maintenance costs		
Lowered stock costs		
Reduced energy costs		
Cost avoidance		
Reduced new personnel requirement		
Eliminate planned new equipment		
Intangible benefits		
Customer goodwill		
Improved decision making		

Figure 5.9 Value chain analysis summary

Another way of looking at this is shown in the box below.

Gaining competitive advantage through value in use

1. *Reduce the life cycle/alter the cost mix*
   Customers are often willing to pay a considerably higher initial price for a product with significantly lower post-purchase costs.

2. *Expand value through functional redesign*
   For example a product that increases the user's production capacity or throughput.

   A product that enables the user to improve the quality or reliability of his or her end product.

   A product that enhances end-use flexibility.

   A product that adds functions or permits added applications.

3. *Expand incremental value by developing associated intangibles*
   For example service, financing, 'prestige'.

An international chemical company undertook this investigation process using a novel method. They organized a two-day event for eight very senior people from different functions in a large packaging company. These executives included marketing people, a health and safety executive, an environmental specialist, a logistics manager, a manufacturing manager and a couple of directors! These executives were matched by equivalent managers and directors from the supplying company. An independent consultant was asked to chair the two-day event.

The purpose of the event, which was held in a neutral location, was to investigate ways in which the several goods and services of the supplying company were received, used and perceived by the customer. This was obviously only possible because of the good relationships already enjoyed by the supplier.

While it took a few hours for the independent moderator to break down the natural barriers to honest and open communication, the event had a major impact on the processes and attitudes of the supplier. For example at one stage, the customers were asked to go into a syndicate room and write down all the things they did not like or found inadequate in the supplying company. The sheer size of the list and the contents so shocked the supplier that it immediately agreed to set up a number of functional and cross-functional working groups comprising executives from both sides to study how cost-effective improvements could be made.

All issues were investigated openly and honestly, ranging from the strategic issues faced by the customer in its industry, to very tactical issues concerned with processes. The end result was a dramatically improved relationship that led to substantial benefits to both sides.

It is not suggested that this is the only way to discover the kind of detailed information outlined in Figure 5.9. In many cases, much patience is required over considerable periods of time and the effectiveness and efficiency with which this investigative task can be carried out will be a function of how good and deep the existing relationships are.

None the less, it is difficult to see how improvements can be made without a deep understanding of the customer's systems and processes.

The list of possibilities for the supplier is now growing quite considerably. But there are still more aspects that need to be analysed.

Step 7 The customer's buying process

Figure 5.10 shows the buying process for goods and services. In the remainder of this section, it will be assumed that we are selling a service.

Selling to an organization can be a complex process because it is possible for a number of different people to become involved at the customer end. Although theoretically only one of these is the buyer, in practice he or she might not be allowed to make any decision to purchase until others with technical expertise or hierarchical responsibility have given their approval.

The personal authority of the buyer will to a large extent be governed by these factors:

1 *The cost of the service* – the higher the cost, the higher in the organization will the purchasing decision be made (see Table 5.1). Please note that, although the level of expenditure figures will have increased substantially during the past fourteen years, the table is included because it is indicative of a hierarchy of purchasing authority.
2 *The 'newness' of the service* – the relative novelty of the service will pose an element of commercial risk for an organization. A new and untried proposition will require support at a senior management level, whereas routine, non-risky service can be handled at a lower level.
3 *The complexity of the service* – the more complex the service offered, the more technical implications have to be understood within the client company. Several specialist managers might be required to give their approval before the transaction can be completed.

All those involved in the buying decision are known as the decision-making unit (DMU), and it is important for the salesperson to identify the DMU in all current and prospective customer companies. Table 5.2 gives some research findings which show how rarely salespeople reach all component members of the DMU.

Customer _____
Address _____

Salesperson _____
Products _____
Telephone number _____
Date of analysis _____
Date of reviews _____

Buy class: New buy   Straight re-buy   Modified re-buy

Member of Decision-Making Unit (DMU) Buy phase Name	Production	Sales & Marketing	Research & Development	Finance & Accounts	Purchasing	Data Processing	Other
1 Recognizes need or problem and works out general solution							
2 Works out characteristics and quantity of what is needed							
3 Prepares detailed specification							
4 Searches for and locates potential sources of supply							
5 Analyses and evaluates tenders, plans, products							
6 Selects supplier							
7 Places order							
8 Checks and tests products							

Factors for consideration

1 price
2 performance
3 availability
4 back-up service
5 reliability of supplier
6 other users' experience
7 guarantees and warranties
8 payment terms, credit or discount
9 other, e.g. past purchases, prestige, image, etc.

Figure 5.10 Buying process for goods and services (adapted from J. Robinson, C.W. Farris and Y. Wind, *Industrial Buying and Creative Marketing*, Allyn and Bacon, 1967)

Table 5.1 Responsibility for financial expenditure

Level of expenditure	Level at which decision is taken			
	Board (collective)	Individual director	Departmental manager	Lower management or clerical
Over £50,000	88%	11%	2%	–
Up to £50,000	70%	25%	4%	Less than 0.5%
Up to £5,000	29%	55%	14%	2%
Up to £2,500	18%	54%	24%	4%
Up to £500	4%	31%	52%	14%

Source: 'How British Industry Buys', a survey conducted by Cranfield School of Management for *The Financial Times*, January 1984

Table 5.2 Buying influences by company size

Number of employees	Average number of buying influences (the DMU)	Average number of contacts made by salesperson
0–200	3.42	1.72
201–400	4.85	1.75
401–1000	5.81	1.90
1000 plus	6.50	1.65

Source: McGraw-Hill

A way of anticipating who would be involved in the decision-making processes in a company is to consider the sales transaction from the buyer's point of view. It has been recognized that the process can be split into a number of distinct steps known as 'buy phases'. These buy phases will be followed in most cases, particularly for major purchases. It will be obvious that at stages beyond the Mid-KAM stage, the incumbent supplier will have an inside track, hence an advantage, throughout the process. In many cases, customers do not even bother to put it out to tender, preferring to deal with their current trusted partner.

Buy phases

(This section of the text owes much to the original research conducted by the Marketing Science Institute in the USA under the guidance of Patrick J. Robinson.)

1 *Problem identification* – a problem is identified or anticipated and a general solution worked out. For example the marketing planning department finds that it has inadequate information about sales records and costs. It needs better information made available on the computer.

2 *Problem definition* – the problem is examined in more detail in order to grasp the dimensions and hence the nature of the ultimate choice of solution. Taking our example further, investigation shows that the original software system was not devised with the current marketing planning requirements in mind. A new system is required which can also provide the option for the inclusion of other new data.

3 *Solution specification* – the various technical requirements are listed and a sum of money is allocated to cover the cost of investing in new software.

4 *Search* – a search is made for potential suppliers. In this case, those with the capability of devising a 'tailor-made' system to meet the above requirements.

5 *Assessment* – proposals from interested suppliers are assessed and evaluated.

6 *Selection* – a supplier is selected and probably final details are negotiated prior to the next step.

7 *Agreement* – a contract/agreement is signed.

8 *Monitoring* – the service is monitored in terms of meeting installation deadlines and performance claims.

If we happened to be running a computer programming service to industry, we could deduce from the above process that the DMU at this company might well contain the following people: marketing planner, sales director, sales office manager, the company computer specialist, the company accountant, the company secretary and perhaps even the managing director, depending on the nature of the contract and the buyer. Sometimes the buyer might be one of those already listed and not exist as a separate role.

We could also speculate with some certainty that each of these people would need to be satisfied about different aspects of the efficiency of our service and we would need to plan accordingly.

For now, it is enough to recognize that when selling to an organization the person with the title of buyer is often unable to make important decisions on their own. Although he or she can be a useful cog in the company's purchasing machine, he or she is often not a free agent.

Pressure on the buyer

When we purchase something for the home we know from our own experience how difficult it can sometimes be. Even if we are only buying a carpet, we have to agree whether or not it should be plain or patterned, what colour, what price, what quality, and so on. Even these considerations are clouded by issues such as whether the neighbours or relatives will think we are copying them, or whether we are being too chic, or too outrageous. The buying decision makers in a typical company are faced with many more pressures than these. They stem from two origins: from outside the company, and from inside.

External pressures

These can be many and various and might include such issues as:

1 *The economic situation* – what will be the cost of borrowing? Are interest rates likely to rise or fall? Is it a good time to invest in a new service now? Is the market decline really over or should we wait for more signals of recovery?
2 *Political considerations* – how will government fiscal policy affect our business or that of our customers? Will proposed legislation have an impact on either us or our markets?
3 *Technology* – how are we as a company keeping up with technological developments? How does this new proposal rate on a technological scale? Is it too near the frontiers of existing knowledge? How long will it be before a whole new phase of technology supersedes this investment?
4 *Environmental considerations* – will this new service be advantageous to us in terms of energy conservation or pollution control? Does it present any increase in hazards to our workforce? Will we need more room to expand? Is such room available?
5 *The business climate* – how do our profit levels compare with those of companies in general and those in our type of business in particular? Are there material cost increases in the pipeline that could reduce our profits? Is the cost of labour increasing?

Any one of these could put pressure on the buying decision maker – and these are only the external pressures.

Internal pressures

Within the company there can be another set of pressures such as:

1 *Confused information* – it is often difficult to obtain the correct information to back up a buying decision. Either the information does not exist, or else it has not been communicated accurately from the specialist department. Sometimes it is not presented in a convenient form and leads to misunderstandings.
2 *Internal politics* – the relative status of individuals or departments can sometimes hinder the buying process. Personal rivalries or vested interests could create difficulties about priorities or standards. The 'politics' might entail non-essential people being involved in the decision-making process, thereby elongating the communication chain and slowing down decision making.
3 *Organizational* – how the company is organized can affect the efficiency of its buying process. It is essential for everyone to be aware of their roles and levels of authority if they are to perform effectively.

Personal pressure

Buyers can be pressurized by a number of personal matters, some real, others imagined. They might be unsure about their role or how their colleagues accept their judgement. They might lack experience in the buying role and be unsure of how to conduct themselves. They might prefer a quiet life and therefore be against change, preferring to continue transactions with tried and tested suppliers – even if it can be clearly demonstrated that there are advantages in changing them. They might be naturally shy and not enjoy first meetings. They might find it difficult to learn new information about technical developments or the special features of your particular service.

All of these pressures, both internal and external, have a profound bearing on the behaviour of the buyer, and if the salesperson is to relate to the buyer, he or she must try to understand them.

By way of summarizing this section on business-to-business selling, it can be demonstrated that the successful salesperson needs to be aware of all these things when approaching a buyer acting on behalf of an organization. The following need to be known and understood.

1 The relative influence of the buyer in the context of the particular product or service being offered.
2 What constitutes the DMU in the buying company.
3 How the buying process works.
4 The pressures on the buying decision maker.

With this information, the salesperson is in a better position to plan his or her work and conduct themselves appropriately when face to face with the buying decision maker(s). Exactly how this information is used will be covered later.

Buy classes

Whether or not the salesperson is selling to an individual or to an organization, he or she can divide the decision-making process of their prospects into what are termed buy classes. There are three types of buy class:

1 *New buy* – in effect all the foregoing discussion has focused on the new buy category. It is here that those people who make up the DMU are fully exercised as the buy phases unfold. It is in the new buy class that the needs of all decision makers need to be met and influenced by the salesperson. Not surprisingly, this takes time and so it is not unusual for a lengthy period to elapse between the initial discussion and landing the contract.
2 *Straight re-buy* – once the salesperson has had the opportunity to demonstrate how the service can help the customer, further purchases of the service do not generally require such a rigorous examination at all of the buy phases. In fact, should the customer merely want a repeat purchase of the same service, then their only concerns are likely to be around issues such as: has the price been held to the same level as before? Will the standard of the service be unchanged? Can it be provided at a specific time? Such issues can generally be resolved by negotiation with the buyer.

3 *Modified re-buy* – sometimes a modification in the product or service might be necessary. It might be that the supplier wants to up-date the product or service and provide better performance by using different methods or equipment. Alternatively, it could be the customer who calls for some form of modification from the original purchase. Whatever the origin, all or some of the buy phases will have to be re-examined, and again the salesperson will have to meet and influence the relevant members of the DMU.

There are often advantages for a salesperson to try and change a straight re-buy into a modified re-buy. They are twofold:

1 A modified re-buy reactivates and strengthens the relationship with the various members of the customer's DMU.
2 The more closely a supplier can match its service to the customer's needs (and remember, this matching only comes about as a result of a mutual learning, as communication and trust develop between the supplier and the customer), the more committed the customer becomes to the service.

The higher the commitment the customer has to the particular service and the supplier, the more difficult it becomes for competitors to break in.

Identifying the buyer

Recognizing that there is a DMU is an important first step for the salesperson, but having done this, it is essential to identify who actually has the power to make the purchase.

Failure to do so will result in much wasted time and frustration. No matter how persuasive the arguments for buying your service, if you are not reaching the key decision maker then all your efforts might be in vain. Finding this person is too important to be left to chance and yet many salespeople fail to meet them. Sometimes they just have not done enough research about the company in order to get an accurate picture of how it operates, its personnel and the key issues that they are concerned with.

Alternatively, many salespeople prefer to continue meeting their original contacts in the client company, the ones with whom they feel comfortable and have come to regard as friends, rather than extending their network of contacts. They fight shy of the risk of meeting the influential people in companies. Because many will hold senior positions, the thought of meeting them somehow seems a daunting prospect, especially to complacent or ill-prepared salespeople.

Yet many of these fears are groundless. There is no evidence that senior executives set out to be deliberately obstructive or use meetings to expose the salesperson's possible inadequacies. In fact, quite the opposite appears to be true.

Certainly, they will be busy people and so will want discussion to be to the point and relevant. At the same time, they will be trying to get the best deal for the company and it is only natural that they should.

Step 8 Your sales history with the client

Figure 5.11 is a very simple analysis of your sales over a designated period of time with this customer and its purpose is merely to summarize the history, share and prospects with the customer.

Your sales history with the client

Products		T–2	T–1	T–0	Trend
Customer volume (Total)					
OUR volume					
OUR share volume					
OUR Share value					

Sales analysis

Products		T–2	T–1	T–0	Trend
	Val				
	Vol				
	%				
	Val				
	Vol				
	%				
	Val				
	Vol				
	%				
	Val				
	Vol				
	%				
	Val				
	Vol				
	%				

Comments

Figure 5.11 Sales analysis and history

Step 9 Competitive comparison and competitor strategy

Figure 5.12 shows one of a number of possible ways of establishing how well you are meeting the customer's needs in comparison with your competitors. It is obviously better if this is done using independent market research evidence, but providing the analysis suggested in this chapter is carried out thoroughly and with diligence, it should be possible to complete this part of the analysis with sufficient accuracy.

Competitive comparison

	Importance rating	You	Competitor 1	2	3	Implications
Product quality						
Product range						
Availability						
Delivery						
Price/discounts						
Terms						
Sales support						
Promotion support						
Other						

Importance rating
(by customer)

A – Very important (essential)
B – Important (desirable)
C – Low importance

Rating
(customer view)

1 – Consistently/fully meets needs
2 – Meets needs inconsistently
3 – Fails to meet needs

Competitor strategy

Competitor	Strategy
1.	
2.	
3.	

Figure 5.12 Competitive comparison and competitor strategy

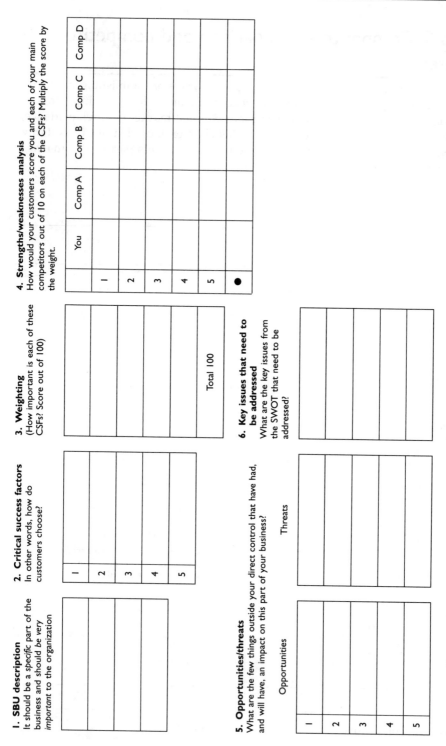

1. SBU description
It should be a *specific* part of the business and should be *very important* to the organization

2. Critical success factors
In other words, how do customers choose?

1	
2	
3	
4	
5	

3. Weighting
(How important is each of these CSFs? Score out of 100)

Total 100	

4. Strengths/weaknesses analysis
How would your customers score you and each of your main competitors out of 10 on each of the CSFs? Multiply the score by the weight.

	You	Comp A	Comp B	Comp C	Comp D
1					
2					
3					
4					
5					
●					

5. Opportunities/threats
What are the few things outside your direct control that have had, and will have, an impact on this part of your business?

Opportunities

1	
2	
3	
4	
5	

Threats

6. Key issues that need to be addressed
What are the key issues from the SWOT that need to be addressed?

Figure 5.13 Strategic marketing planning exercise – SWOT analysis (from M.H.B. McDonald, *Marketing Plans: how to prepare them; how to use them*, Butterworth-Heinemann, 1996)

Some people prefer to carry out this analysis using a more traditional SWOT format (strengths, weaknesses, opportunities and threats). Such an analysis is shown in Figure 5.13.

The main point, of course, is that any organization hoping to get and keep the business with a major account needs to provide superior customer value and this can only be achieved by comparisons with the best the competitors have to offer.

Next steps

The painstaking analysis is now complete and a number of customer critical success factors (CSFs) will have been accumulated, together with specific ways in which your products or services and processes can help.

Figure 5.14 is a useful way of categorizing your solutions and approaches to your client prior to producing a strategic marketing plan for the customer, which will be explained later in this chapter.

The applications portfolio shows four boxes. The bottom left and right boxes are labelled AVOIDING DISADVANTAGE. While the meaning of this label might be self evident, it is none the less worth giving an example of this category. Take, for example a bank buying automatic telling machines for use by customers outside bank opening hours. Not having them would clearly place the bank at a disadvantage. However, having them does not give the bank any advantage either. The majority of commercial transactions fall into this category. The

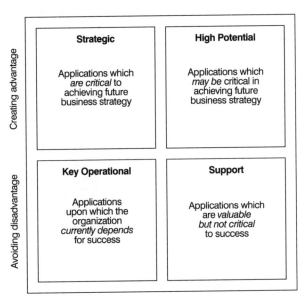

Figure 5.14 The applications portfolio

bottom left box represents key operational activities, such as basic accounting, manufacturing and distribution systems. The bottom right box might include activities such as producing overhead slides for internal presentations.

In contrast, the top two boxes represent a real opportunity to differentiate your organization's offering by creating advantage for the customer. The top right box might be beta testing a product, service, or process prior to making a major investment in launching it for the customer. A classic example of this was Thompson's computer systems in the leisure/holiday market.

The reality of commercial life is that most of what any organization does falls into the former category. Leading companies, however, work hard at developing products, services and processes designed to create advantage for their major accounts, for it is clear that such suppliers will always be preferred over those who merely offer 'me too' products and trade only on price.

The strategic marketing plan for key accounts

We saw in Chapter 3 what the contents of a strategic marketing plan are. These are repeated here.

Contents of the strategic marketing plan

Mission statement

Financial summary

Market overview   Market structure
                                         Market trends
                                         Key market segments
                                         Gap analysis

Opportunities and threats   By product
                                         By segment
                                         Overall

Strengths and weaknesses   By product
                                         By segment
                                         Overall

Portfolio summary

Assumptions

Marketing objectives   Strategic focus
                                         Product mix
                                         Product development
                                         Product deletion
                                         Market extension
                                         Target customer groups

Marketing strategies   Product
                                         Price
                                         Promotion
                                         Place

Resource requirements

The contents of a key account strategic marketing plan are shown below.

The contents of a key account strategic marketing plan (T+3)

Mission/purpose statement
Financial summary
Key account overview
Client's CSF analyses summary
Applications portfolio summary
Assumptions
Objectives and strategies
Budget

The mission/purpose statement

While this is not essential in all cases, it is useful if the person preparing the plan makes at least a brief statement about the position of this particular key account in the organization's key account portfolio. For example, if the account is in the top right-hand box of Figure 5.2, an investment plan is called for, while one in the bottom right-hand box would call for a transaction-by-transaction approach, with each one justified on the basis of net free cash flow. Those in the top left-hand box require an investment approach, but one requiring an acceptable profit. Finally, those in the bottom left-hand box should be managed for sustained profits, using prudence and management judgement.

It is important that these expectations should be verbalized up front in the plan in order to make clear the strategic context of the plan that follows.

Financial summary

This is merely a graphical representation of the revenue and costs for the three years of the plan. It is in effect a summary of the more detailed budget that appears later in the plan.

Key account overview

This is somewhat like a market overview and should contain a summary of the more important facts about the customer's markets, competitors and prospects.

Client's CSF analyses summary

This brings together the client's critical success factors that have emerged from the earlier analysis.

The applications portfolio summary

This, as explained above, categorizes your solutions according to their importance to the client's business.

Assumptions

As in a strategic marketing plan, this specifies the conditions necessary for the plan to happen. They should be few in number and key.

Objectives and strategies

Figures 5.15, 5.16 and 5.17 set out objectives and strategies for the key account.

Products		Last year	T + I	T + 2	T + 3
	Val				
	Vol				
	%				
	Val				
	Vol				
	%				
	Val				
	Vol				
	%				
	Val				
	Vol				
	%				
	Val				
	Vol				
	%				
	Val				
	Vol				
	%				

Figure 5.15 Objectives sales

Other objectives
(consider customer attitude, customer training, new product/application development and customer's business performance improvements

_____

_____

_____

_____

_____

_____

_____

_____

_____

Figure 5.16 Other objectives

Products	Strategy

In developing strategy consider:

Product	include new products/quality/product mix/technical service/literature
Price	include pricing against competition/volume vs. price/terms and conditions
Place	include packaging/lot sizes/distribution/customer service
Promotion	include entertainment/advertising/displays, etc.

Figure 5.17 Strategy

The budget

This will be in accordance with the particular requirements of the supplying organization and should set out the details of revenues and costs during the three-year planning period.

Action programme and account review

Figures 5.18 and 5.19 complete the circle and translate the key account strategic marketing plan into a more detailed scheduling and costing out of the specific actions to achieve the first year of the plan, together with their regular review.

Month	Objective and main activities
January	
February	
March	
April	
May	
June	
July	
August	
September	
October	
November	
December	

Support required (technical, management, etc.)

Figure 5.18 Action programme

Month	Activity to review	With whom
January		
February		
March		
April		
May		
June		
July		
August		
September		
October		
November		
December		

Figure 5.19 Account review

Final thoughts

Research at Cranfield has shown that very few companies prepare strategic marketing plans for their key accounts. It is hoped that this chapter has succeeded in indicating that the process is complex and time consuming. Yet, without all this dedicated effort, it is unlikely that any supplier will be able to provide superior value to its key accounts and hence achieve sustainable competitive advantage.

Chapter 6

The role and skills of the key account manager

Introduction

The chapter explains how the role of the key account manager evolves with the selling company/buying company relationship, and presents the wide portfolio of skills expected of key account managers at partnership and synergistic levels and how they might be developed. It also discusses issues of status and reward. Finally, there is a short introduction to the key account manager's responsibilities in developing others in the key account team.

The role of the key account manager is critical, not just to selling companies, but to buying companies as well. Buying companies have a lot to gain from excellence in key account management, and those in partnership relationships with suppliers are increasingly relying on it. Of course, the selling company has all the challenges in terms of recruiting and developing key account managers, and ensuring key account management skills pervade their whole organization.

This chapter examines first of all the changing nature of the expectations of key account managers at the different stages in the KAM relational development model. The formula for developing the 'ideal' key account manager is then explored, followed by an examination of the implications of that high level of skill on status and rewards. Finally, the role of key account teams in spreading key account management skills throughout the selling company is discussed.

The role of the key account manager – evolving with the supplier/customer relationship

The role of the key account manager differs according to the position of the seller/buyer relationship in the relationship development model. This does not mean to say that the key account manager has to be changed as the relationship evolves. Many key account managers have grown in stature with their accounts. In other cases, senior key account managers are tasked with converting a key prospect so that they can revisit the skills required in new business, and ensure the rapid development of that business.

Pre-KAM

Buying company expectations
At the Pre-KAM stage, the buying company is expecting the selling company to do all the running for their business. The decision makers expect key account managers first and foremost to demonstrate product and/or service superiority, so a thorough understanding of the product is critical. To have to haul in a specialist at such an early stage would indicate superficiality. He or she will also be expected to convey an understanding of how the product/service can be applied in the buying company's business to help it to achieve competitive edge.

Buying company decision makers demand that the key account manager seeks them out, to persuade them to make time for a meeting and then to maximize the time made available to impress them with a vision of better business. So communications and presentation skills are critical. Key account managers must convince the decision makers that they want to make them happy as much as they want to make their own manager happy! Persistence will be essential, and negotiation skills will be needed even to get into decision makers' diaries. In pursuit of these qualities, many key account managers come from a sales background.

Selling company focus
Although there is an emphasis on selling skills at the Pre-KAM stage, all key accounts and prospects deserve a long-term perspective. A key account manager is rarely, if ever, involved in 'hard' selling. The key account manager and the selling company must demonstrate that they are initiating the relationship for the long term. Therefore, the distinction between the concept of 'streetwise' negotiation and principled negotiation must be made.

Streetwise negotiation, the game of winning as much as you can, potentially at the expense of the prospect, is totally out of place in the selling company that has embraced key account management as a way of doing business. Principled negotiation, based upon theories of rational decision making, was originally defined by Harvard lawyers Roger Fisher and Bill Ury. It is based on objective criteria and the search for options for mutual gain.

Recruiting a key account is even more difficult than recruiting a key account manager! Having decided on the balances of power, risk and trust in the potential relationship, the manager of key account managers will have chosen a key account manager to suit this prospect. Assumptions will have been made about levels of knowledge and skills required and personality matches. The key account manager must be able to identify conversion opportunities, demonstrate entrepreneurial flair and business 'nous'.

Background activity of the key account manager at this stage

Before dedicating resources to the prospect, the selling company must be convinced that the probability of a profitable relationship is high. The key account manager must prepare a credible long-term plan for establishing this company as a key account, perhaps even as a partner within the timeframe of the plan, which should be 3–5 years. Research on the prospect is needed – what is their financial position, their strategy? What external factors are impacting them (e.g. legislation, new technology)? What market segments do they serve? Who are their competitors? After research, the potential of the account and the selling company's capabilities in realizing it can be analysed.

Developing a long-term view is very important – while the key account manager is indeed hunting at the Pre-KAM stage, he or she also has to act as the guardian of the environment for the next generation of business activity as well.

Early-KAM

Buying company expectations

The key account manager needs to understand how the key account is motivated. What are the things which made them choose this selling company, and how can those factors be strengthened further?

If the buying company bought on price, and the decision makers' intentions do not include anything more than regular transactions, the key account manager will be stuck with demonstrating basic skills such as technical knowledge of the product or service and occasional negotiations. The relationships will not progress beyond Early-KAM.

If there is more potential, the key account manager's challenges become more difficult once the business is won. The customer will probably have opted for a trial period, pilot, or limited term contract in order to give the selling company an opportunity to prove itself. Even if expectations have been set realistically, the buying company is probably hoping for immediately noticeable improvements. The key account manager may be swamped with technical queries and will have to ensure he or she can answer them or someone else can answer them quickly. A lot of time must also be spent with the customer, seeing how the product is being used, and making contact with people at all levels.

Above all, the key account manager must convince and reassure the buying company's decision makers that they have made the right decision.

The key account manager must also establish integrity – what has been promised must be delivered. However, an individual can only deliver what it is in his or her power to deliver. The whole company must believe in demonstrating integrity or relationships with customers will never progress and will eventually fail. The key account manager needs the support of the rest of the company – operations, logistics, accounts, etc. in order to make sure the customer is satisfied.

This may sound so obvious, and yet integrity is perceived to be at a premium. Buying companies emphasize the priority they attach to it, and their frequent perception that suppliers are not up to it. Selling companies who aspire to integrity simply have to ask their business partners what promises they value, and set out a programme to achieve them. Integrity is a quality, but it is possible to identify fundamental items of evidence of it. The supplier who consistently delivers to customers accurately and on time is displaying trustworthiness where it matters most. The keeping of promises which affect the business success of each party in the business relationship can be measured and should be measured.

The manner of making promises is also important, hence the distinction previously made between streetwise negotiation and principled negotiation. The ultimate test of integrity, however, is the way in which a failure to deliver a promise is handled. An immediate apology and an offer of compensation may enhance the loyalty of the buying company. Such a policy may be critical at the Early-KAM stage.

Selling company focus

The business must be secured for the long term. The manager of the key account manager will recognize the need for support, and add weight to the key account manager's requirements for resources to fix problems. Nevertheless, it will be expected that the key account manager can convince his or her own colleagues of the importance of this account, and demonstrate leadership in getting responses.

Background activity of the key account manager at this stage

The key account manager will be concentrating on a lot of detail, while also having to keep greater aims in mind. The detail will be mostly about how the product/service works. Exercising personal persuasion, especially with colleagues who can help with technical issues, will be a daily activity, involving explaining why something should be done, offering encouragement and showing appreciation. Administrative and organizational nous will be required in order to get things done. The key account manager will also have to demonstrate listening skills to the buying company, and leadership in suggesting and implementing solutions.

This portfolio of skills is quite a contrast from the selling role. In some companies in the past, once a prospect was converted into a customer, the salesperson handed over to a project manager to establish and develop the business. However, that wastes the rapport that they have established and creates an impression of 'walking away'. A key account manager ought to be able to win business and project manage it.

Mid-KAM

Buying company expectations

The product is right, the price is right, and the buying company wants to do more business with this supplier. In which case, buying company decision makers expect to be recognized as very important to that supplier. A strong association will have been built up with the key account manager – and the buying company will be keenly interested in how highly the selling company regards him or her. In choosing a preferred supplier, they might reasonably expect that their key account manager would have direct access to senior management. They might judge that by how often senior managers are brought in to see them. The buying company's decision makers need a key account manager with the clout to get things done for them, but there will also be a wider perspective. The whole key account team will assume importance to the buying company, as contacts have to be established at all levels between supplier and customer in order to handle the increasing scale of the business between them.

Buying companies will be reluctant to progress a supplier to 'preferred' status if they perceive that the key account manager lacks authority within his or her own organization. Lack of named contacts in other departments would also indicate weakness in the supplier's approach. Some degree of key account teamwork, however informal, ought to be established at this stage.

Selling company focus

Account penetration is all at this stage in the relational model, and preferred supplier status is the goal. The key account manager will be expected to have established the selling company's credentials and is now selling again, perhaps to other divisions or departments within the buying company. The key account manager will be seeking out the competition wherever they are active in the account, and devising strategies to win more business. Things can go wrong at this stage and sensitivity will have to be exercised. Some buying companies never single source, in which case a certain amount of co-existence with competition has to be accepted. The customer may even request competing suppliers to work together on projects or problem resolution.

Background activity of the key account manager at this stage

The social skills of the key account manager will be heavily used at this stage to gain the network within the buying company which will extend the selling company's presence in the account. Gaining credibility and demonstrating authority with contacts across different divisions, further up and further down the company, will be the priority activity. Organizing social events enabling selling company and buying company staff to meet and mix will be one of the mechanisms used. Building morale of the people in other departments of the selling company who deal with the buying company's requirements is also important. It is desirable to establish an informal or semi-formal multidisciplinary team to improve the service to this particular customer.

The key account manager will also be learning more about the buying company, such as the culture of the organization and the impact of changes in the business environment on its activities. He or she will be preparing to demonstrate a full range of financial, marketing and consultancy skills to this customer in order to move the relationship to the partnership stage.

Partnership-KAM

Buying company expectations
The shift away from key account selling and into key account management is complete at the partnership stage. Ensuring mutually agreed performance criteria are met will be a major part of the key account manager's day-to-day responsibilities.

At a strategic level, the key account manager will be producing long-term plans jointly with the key decision makers in the buying company. There will also be concentrated effort to improve processes between the two companies, an activity which can provide a bridge to the next stage of the relational development model.

The buying company is also looking for further demonstration of the selling company's esteem, such as introducing new products or services to them at the test stage, so that they can gain maximum advantage from them as soon as possible.

Selling company focus
Selling company strategists assume that at this stage, the key account manager will be frequently active at very high levels in the buying company, fulfilling a strategic role. The emphasis has switched from gaining volume of business to ensuring even more quality of business and reducing the costs of doing business together.

A high level of skill is involved in managing partnership relationships with key customers, and key account strategists want a range of skills which they admit are almost unattainable. By this stage, the key account manager is neither a hunter nor a farmer, but is conducting an orchestra.

Background activity of the key account manager at this stage
The key account manager must be aware of the latest thinking in business and developing ideas to present to the buying company. The challenges of process improvement will probably dominate the research.

Synergistic-KAM

Buying company expectations
At the synergistic stage, it can simply be stated that the buying company treats the selling company as integral to its efforts to deliver value to its own customers.

Selling company focus
At the synergistic stage, the improvement and integration of processes are all-important, and this will require the key account manager to have an in-depth understanding of process design and the potential of information technology.

Background activity of the key account manager at this stage
Vigilance, monitoring and measuring will be critical, as the 'partnership index' might include up to 200 performance criteria as more and more processes are scrutinized. Achieving them should be business as usual for the selling company, the key account manager is primarily concerned with resolving exceptions.

The key account manager must also maintain a broad perspective, particularly to ensure that the selling company could withstand any market test the buying company might choose to impose, wherever and whenever it came. Both analytical and creative thinking skills will be required to secure the longevity of the synergistic relationship.

Table 6.1 provides a summary of the role of the key account manager.

In seller/buyer relationships unlikely to progress beyond the early stages of KAM the emphasis will be on basic skills for key account managers, skills such as technical knowledge of the products and selling/negotiation skills.

From Mid-KAM through to Synergistic-KAM, key account managers are business managers with a full range of financial, marketing and consultancy skills, and high status and authority with both their own employers and within their key account. Very highly skilled individuals are required to develop accounts to the partnership or synergistic stage and keep them there. In fact, key account strategists would say that the full complement of skills is almost unattainable in any one individual.

The key account managers in a services company were all highly educated, highly professional managers in charge of global teams of up to 100 other professionals, who in turn were managing teams of operatives. The global key account managers reported directly to the general manager.

By the time sales professionals are ready for key accounts, they are already aspiring to line management, but downsizing and delayering in companies has

Table 6.1 Summary – the role of the key account manager – evolving with the supplier/customer relationship

	Pre-KAM	Early-KAM	Mid-KAM	Partnership-KAM	Synergistic-KAM
Buying company view	Product knowledge – technical Product knowledge – applications Communications	Product knowledge – technical Integrity	Authority of the key account manager Key account management team assumes importance	Performance monitoring Long-term planning Process review	Supplier as integral strategic resource
Selling company focus	Selling and negotiation	Internal negotiation	Account penetration	Quality improvement and cost reduction	Process integration
Key account manager's background activities	Research and planning	Administration Attention to detail Getting things done	Social skills/ networking Learning more about the customer	Thinking skills Research	Exception handling Prepare for market testing

reduced those career opportunities. Key account management has to accrue high status in order to be attractive in the long term to ambitious professionals.

Development of key account management skills

There is much diversity of opinion on the desirable skills and qualities of a key account manager. Buying company contacts value integrity and technical product knowledge very highly, followed by knowledge of their business; while selling and negotiating skills are important to key account managers themselves. Administrative, strategic and leadership skills appear to be valued more by key account strategists in selling companies than by the buying company contacts, although this is likely to change as customers reveal a greater reliance on supplier expertise due to rationalizing their own resources. Table 6.2 illustrates the key skills and qualities of key account managers.

Table 6.2 The key skills and qualities of key account managers

	Buying company view	Selling company strategic view	Key account manager's view
1st	Integrity	Knowledge of business environment	Selling/negotiating
2nd	Understanding our business	Communications	Communications
3rd	Product knowledge – technical	Strategic thinking	Understanding customer's business
4th	Product knowledge – applications	Selling/negotiating	Strategic thinking
5th	Communications	Product knowledge – technical	Technical/financial/ markets/credibility

The nearest we can get to definition of the ideal key account manager, 'the unattainable', would be a collection of all the skills and qualities desired by selling companies and buying companies at higher relational levels. To fulfil all their expectations, the key account manager needs:

● *Personal qualities*
    integrity
    resilience/persistent
    selling/negotiating
    'likeability'
● *Subject knowledge*
    product knowledge – technical and applications in the customer's business
    understanding the business environment, markets
    financial
    legal
    computer literacy
    languages/cultural
● *Thinking skills*
    creativity and flexibility
    strategic thinking/planning
    'boundary spanning'
● *Managerial skills*
    communication skills including listening, persuasion
    people management/leadership
    credibility – boardroom to postroom
    administration/organization

Personal qualities

These can perhaps be developed, but most companies would probably want to buy them in. The raw materials required in a key account manager are integrity, persistence, selling and negotiating skills and 'likeability'.

Integrity

Buying company decision makers emphasize the importance of being able to trust the key account manager as an individual, as well as expecting selling companies to demonstrate corporate integrity. Delivering on promises has already been described in some detail. The difficulty faced by key account managers, even at this basic level of skill and even at the earliest stages of KAM, is the perceived paradox between integrity and selling. Buying company decision makers express their distaste at being sold to. How can selling be reconciled with integrity?

Resilience and persistence

The need for the key account manager to be resilient is noticed mostly by their managers, who seem to be more conscious of the strains of the job than key account managers or buying company decision makers. There ought to be no doubt that the role requires mental strength. Especially at the early stages, the key account manager may not be able to achieve what they have set out to do very quickly. Customer acceptance often takes longer than anticipated. Resilience and persistence are needed.

Selling and negotiating

It is necessary for the selling company recruiting a key account manager to move away from the popular view of selling, and think of the key account manager in terms of a secular evangelist. It is not just shifting boxes for the sake of a bonus – it is about promoting a product because it is believed that it can help the customer to achieve long-term objectives. Selling in this context can be associated with integrity and persistence.

'Selling' actually takes up a small proportion of a key account manager's time, it may be as little as 10 per cent of the key account manager's activity in a mature seller/buyer relationship. Selling effort also depends on the pace at which the selling company is introducing new products. Nevertheless, key account managers believe that a key account manager who forgets about selling is heading for trouble. Their job is about making money for the selling company, and they need to invest some emotion in that, even though they recognize the importance of a 'soft' sales approach.

'Likeability'

Buying company decision makers talk a lot about the 'likeability' of various suppliers' key account managers. Issues of personal chemistry or fit clearly do play some part in the successful achievement of account objectives. A buying company decision maker might make sure that the conditions were not right for doing business if he or she did not like the key account manager.

Selling companies ought to consider ways of getting the personality types of key account managers to match their main buying company contacts, but since changes must take place from time to time, it can hardly be an infallible science.

Key account managers are conscious of the importance of personal fit, but expect that buying company decision makers will demonstrate professionalism and have a wide interpretation of it. If the main contact were a jigsaw piece, there might be four to five key account manager pieces which would fit around them. Obvious mismatches, such as a young Oxbridge graduate with someone proud of their street credibility, can be easily avoided. Sometimes, suppliers offer key account managers on 'trial' to see if the buying company likes them. Usually, buying company decision makers note that preferred and partnership suppliers always offer personable people.

'Likeability' cannot be easily defined, but selling companies need to exercise care in recruiting confidence but not arrogance, customer care but not obsequiousness, and communication skills which include listening and sociability. Care must also be taken to ensure that personality profiling has no adverse impact on equal opportunities.

Subject knowledge

Subject knowledge can clearly be taught to anyone with reasonable intelligence and concentration span, yet many companies feel that key account managers do not know enough abut products, markets and business in general. Facts can be learnt from books, tapes, videos (distance learning). This is the easiest aspect of developing key account managers, and one which can have immediate results in terms of improving customer satisfaction.

Product knowledge – technical

There is no doubt, especially in the early stages of KAM, that it is very important for the key account manager to be able to handle technical questions. A majority of the buying company's technical questions ought to be within the key account manager's span of knowledge, although a minority of buying companies place more emphasis on the key account manager being able to get things done and knowing where to get the technical back up and how to apply it to their need. Access to technical databases might be an expedient support tool.

In the early days of question and answer databases, information systems companies had a great opportunity to demonstrate to key accounts how they practised what they preached. Account managers would receive telephone calls from customers about almost anything, and could turn to their screens, enter a few key words and, usually, find an answer for them. They did not need to be technically expert on every aspect of the customer's installation, provided they were expert at searching the databases!

Product knowledge – applications

Besides knowing the features of a product, how it works and what it does for a customer are even more important. It would be difficult for a key account manager to be successful without a thorough understanding of the buying company's business and how the product can be applied to their best advantage. This is a relatively new requirement. Due to downsizing, buying companies are more reliant on the key account manager to know enough about their business to be able to present the customer specific benefits of their solutions.

Market/business knowledge

Following on from understanding the buying company's business, knowledge of the industry in which the buying company works is also required. Buying companies want the key account manager to know as much about the political, economic, social and technological factors affecting their business as they know themselves.

'We have to admit, our key account manager knows more about our business environment than we do . . .' A buying company decision maker acknowledging part of what made a particular supplier strategically important.

Financial

The ability to present a sound financial case within a proposal is recognized as important by most key account strategists, and is certainly missed by buying companies when it is not available. Buying companies say that they would value more financial input from suppliers, although the willingness of the supplier to provide is dependent on the customer's willingness to reciprocate. Regardless of how much reciprocity can be achieved, principled negotiation is not possible if the key account manager does not understand the whole financial picture, especially the link between activities and cost.

Legal

Although contracts are ultimately in the hands of lawyers, it is helpful for the key account manager to understand the basics of commercial law, including contract law, employment law, competition law and consumer protection law. For a global key account manager, the priority need is to understand the legal framework of the country whose laws govern agreements between the selling company and the buying company in addition to the laws of the country in which he or she is based.

Computer literacy and appreciation of information systems

Use of information technology is a prerequisite skill for business these days, and almost a fourth essential alongside the 3Rs in schools. Key account managers should use information systems, especially for communications within the selling company and externally. They must also be aware of the potential for information systems to improve selling company and buying company integration.

Cultural skills and languages

The greatest errors in military history have been made because the strategists failed to understand the point of view of their opponents. In modern business strategy, quality can be achieved by acquiring a thorough understanding of the customer's point of view as well as competitors. This quality must encompass a variety of national and corporate cultures.

Facts can be learnt about doing business in different parts of the world. This is the first step to acquiring an understanding of cultural diversity and other people's points of view.

Language can be taught as well. Governments have programmes to teach fluency in a vast variety of languages. Diplomats are immersed in the language of their new postings, sometimes before they even start any other research about the country. Businesses which are serious about global reach will also train professionals to be great communicators in languages other than their own.

Thinking skills

The assumption is usually made that the key account managers of today are of sufficient intelligence and educational attainment to have well-honed analytical thinking skills. In addition, key account managers need to practice intuitive thinking skills, and these are more difficult to develop. Techniques can be introduced which will help the key account managers expand their capabilities.

Creativity and flexibility

Buying companies value key account managers who are full of ideas for mutual business development and they are critical of key account managers who display a lack of flexibility. Brainstorming is a limited technique when customers are demanding innovative problem-solving initiatives. How to question and to reconfigure situations can be taught, and the use of analogy and scenario planning to build solutions.

Strategic thinking and long-term planning

The process of compiling strategic, long-term plans can also be taught, and the more it is practised the more likely it is that the key account manager will be always able to maintain a long-term view, even when engaged on today's tactical detail. The planning process incorporates establishing the company's mission and financial performance challenges; followed by researching the business environment, customer and competitor activity. This review leads into analyses which will indicate the strategic directions with the highest probability of success.

Strategic planning is done for the account, contributing to the selling company's overall corporate plan; and with the customer, to whatever degree they are prepared to share. The planning process needs to be revisited at least annually, and the plan produced reviewed at least quarterly.

'Boundary spanning'

Key account strategists often worry about key account managers identifying more closely with their customer than they do with their employer, a phenomenon sometimes crudely described as 'going native'. It is understood that this is more likely to occur when the customer ascribed high value to the key account manager who does not have much status or authority within his or her own organization. Such a situation leads the key account manager to identify more closely with the customer's point of view than that of his or her own employer.

It is essential that the key account manager should be able to see situations from more than one point of view, but also be able to control from which point of view he or she is working and to decide on its appropriateness. This skill is called boundary spanning. Sometimes, the key account manager is working on a situation from their manager's point of view, sometimes from the point of view of an individual within the buying company, sometimes as an unbiased external observer and sometimes as an end customer.

In fact, breaking out of the mono-culture of one's own company can offer a wide and powerful spectrum of understanding. A top key account manager will be able to appreciate diversity of behaviours and business styles, springing from different philosophies and historical perspectives. The hopes and fears of the customer, their pride and prejudice and all aspects of their internal frames of reference can be grasped as well as their policies and processes. A truly successful manager needs to 'feel' as well as to know.

It is important for the key account manger to be able to step into someone else's shoes, but also to step out of them. Role playing is taught in drama schools every day. It is not necessary for the key account manager to be an accomplished actor, merely to understand the basics of changing mindset in order to solve problems and set strategy.

Empathy with other points of view can also be achieved through job swaps. This is quite common within selling companies, but has also been successful between selling and buying companies. Usually job swapping has to be practised early in a potential key account manager's career, before he or she has responsibility for a major account.

Managerial skills

It has been emphasized in this book that the key account manager is indeed a manager. Therefore, management skills are required which may partially be taught but must also be facilitated within the selling company, e.g. by mentoring and by practice.

Communication skills including listening

The importance of verbal fluency, presentation skills, and exercising influence in meetings are widely appreciated by all involved in key account relationships. Advanced interpersonal skills are considered a 'must' for key account managers. These can be introduced to aspiring key account managers on courses, but they will also need abundant opportunities to practise them within the selling company before practising them on customers.

Buying company decision makers are very emphatic that listening skills are distinct from other communication skills. Some key account managers can present their products beautifully, but cannot absorb the buying company's response or put themselves in the buying company's position in order to appreciate their priorities. Of course, it is also vital to be able to listen to all members of the key account team.

Leadership/people management

In order to motivate dotted line teams and get things done for the customer, key account managers must demonstrate leadership skills within their own companies, and promote the key account internally. They may also need to lead people in the buying company organization in project situations, or cross-boundary focus teams.

Credibility from the boardroom to the postroom

In a mature seller/buyer relationship, the key account manager is not just convincing purchasing professionals, but must gain buying company commitment at board level.

Key account managers and buying companies also recognize the need to command respect from anyone in either the selling company or buying company organization, at whatever level, who had a direct interest in their solutions.

Administration/organization

The attention to detail required to administer and organize key account activity is the least glamorous aspect of a key account manager's job, but is very important to their managers and is usually quite helpful to the customer as well. These tasks are best understood from a mentoring arrangement – a junior key account manager learning from someone with long and successful experience of what matters.

Status and reward

Status

Assuming the perfect key account manager has been moulded, it seems obvious that he or she will expect high status and rewards commensurate with their strategic importance to the company and the skills and experience they have to apply to their job.

With all the skills and qualities that a key account manager needs to have, what decisions should he or she be able to make? On day-to-day things, buying companies expect an answer on the spot, and they expect more straight talking than they think they get. Often, there is a mismatch of perceptions – the buying company complaining that the key account manager had to take almost every question back to the general manager, while the general manager in that supplier thinks that the key account managers rarely have to take anything back to him or her for approval.

Buying company contacts expect the key account manager to be able to get things done – 'nothing less'. He or she has to be a decision maker. They expect fast responses, and for key account managers to have enough status to be able to achieve things for their customer within their own organization.

Buying companies' expectations of the authority that their key account manager should have sometimes exceed the willingness of selling companies to empower the key account manager. Buying companies think that key account managers should have more resources at their disposal, while selling companies defend the key account manager's need to negotiate for resources for the buying company within the organization.

Key account managers are acutely aware that buying company contacts do not like referral, as they feel the pressure to make decisions and commit their company even when they do not have authority to do so – and sure enough they perceive that the key account manager has total responsibility when things go wrong!

The personal authority of the key account manager depends on the behaviour of others in the selling company organization, above them and below them. If the key account manager is not afforded due deference, even from directors, buying company contacts will be disappointed.

Status is also a matter of symbols. Key account managers are status conscious, and when any one key account manager may be responsible for delivering up to 25 per cent of a company's revenue, it is hardly surprising that they expect symbols of recognition. In most business-to-business selling companies, key account management is more important than general marketing, which is in line with the views of buying companies that general marketing is less important compared to their relationship with the key account manager in terms of delivering business.

Sometimes the status of key account managers in their own company is derived from the relative size and power of their key account. For example, in fast-moving consumer goods suppliers, key account managers for the top few supermarkets have the highest status among their peers.

Status is also derived from the quality of the infrastructure support provided with the role. Key account managers expect powerful cars, equipped with all the paraphernalia of an executive who spends a lot of time on the road. Office equipment at home, such as faxes and computer terminals, also contribute to status as well as productivity. Key account managers also need to be very visible in terms of internal communications, such as the company magazine. Photo opportunities, such as presenting awards, are part of the status mix.

Reward

Most sales professionals with the title key account manager are still paid on the simple basis of salary plus commission. Sales targets are set by sales managers and up to 50 per cent of the key account manager's earnings may depend upon the target being achieved.

Selling companies who practise strategic key account management reward key account managers on a variety of salary and performance criteria, many involving numerical targets. For example one-third personal performance, one-third key account management team performance or unit performance, and one-third corporate performance. Some key account managers are partly rewarded according to customer satisfaction ratings (on their satisfaction with the selling company as a whole as well as the personal performance of their main contact). Sales-based bonuses, market share-based bonuses and profit-based bonuses all figure in the potential array of awards for key account managers.

Key account managers may be motivated by company share price if high value share options are available to them. Others grapple with complicated reward packages based on the accuracy of their forecasting, their recovery of debt, handling of complaints, numbers of new contacts, and opportunities identified. Key account managers whose products are project based may be rewarded on achievement of milestones and deadlines. In industries marked by cyclical sales, such as capital equipment, key account managers may be paid on the value of the key account's portfolio of the selling company's products.

Whatever the mechanism, selling companies with a key account management philosophy want to move key account managers away from counting their commission to concentrating on the customer's long-term interests. Also, some sales managers believe that it is unfair to judge key account managers on revenue if they are looking after only one or two key accounts. The customer's market position may slip, or the main contact's budget may be cut for reasons beyond the key account manager's control. No performance system can make allowances for external impacts. As a result, a significant minority of key account managers are rewarded with 100 per cent salary, although performance measures are still important. High achievement would accelerate promotion.

Table 6.3 Reward mechanisms for key account managers

Reward mechanism	Pros	Cons
100% salary	No constraints to long-term, strategic view No penalties for single account key account managers	Has to be set at a very high threshold in order to be competitive May be demotivating to entrepreneurial personalities
51–80% salary, small percentage bonuses (increasingly believed to be the most suitable and effective)	Key account manager receives some reward associated with particular performance criteria, but can also take a long-term view	A plethora of small bonuses may be complicated to calculate and introduce a hassle factor They may not be sufficient to drive particular activities
30–50% salary, majority PRP (performance-related pay)	Key account manager receives high rewards associated with particular performance criteria which can drive the business	Selection of the appropriate PRP criteria may not be apparent in advance The PRPs may not have a long enough term perspective
Mix of salary and company performance-based bonuses	Promotes interest in teamwork Promotes interest in overall company performance	The company bonus may be too remote from day-to-day activity to be motivating A good performer may be poorly paid when the company overall has a bad patch
50% salary, 50% commission	Direct relationship between sales achievement and reward Drives activity	May not be in customers' best interests The customer may try to exploit this arrangement in sales negotiations

However, a substantial salary with a minority proportion of performance-related pay is emerging as the preferred formula in many companies with partnership relationships. Evidence is mounting that it is the most effective reward mechanism for key account managers, ensuring long-term and short-term success with customers.

Table 6.3 summarizes the different types of reward schemes.

Developing people within key account teams

The use of key account teams to support customers and develop tomorrow's key account managers is becoming more widespread. Customers expect named contacts at all levels and in all relevant departments of a supplier, and the organization of these named individuals into informal or semi-formal teams starts to create synergy on the customer's behalf. It also provides a mechanism for development of key account skills throughout the company. If the key account manager is the sole reason for loyalty between a selling company and buying company, this suggests vulnerability to breakdown and indicates that the relationship is not very mature.

In most companies, even where key account management has been established for many years, teams remain 'dotted line'. This means that the key account manager has the opportunity within the team to develop his or her motivational and leadership skills. The key account manager is leader of the team and places requirements on individuals to achieve things for the customer, but ultimately has little direct influence over their career. Team members will probably have some customer specific objectives, and it is up to the key account manager to help them to achieve them as well as responding to the customer's agenda.

A junior key account manager or trainee can join a key account team in an administrative role to learn from the senior key account manager leading the team. In time they will take over their own key accounts, and the team mechanism can be used to introduce them gradually to the customers. The new key account manager must be given the time to glean the knowledge and know-how from which they derive their credibility. Buying companies certainly appreciate linkage between old and new account managers – it promotes a sense of continuity.

The key account team must be multidisciplinary. Its whole purpose is to ensure that all corners of the selling company appreciate the value of that key account and are working towards improving performance in that account. It is essential that staff from finance, logistics, operations, information technology and product development are included. Depending on the nature of the selling company, merchandising, human resources and purchasing might also be represented.

Within the team itself, members can practise team roles, as well as helping others to understand their specialisms. Rotas can be established for the roles of facilitator, progress chaser, researcher and recorder. The spirit of mutual encouragement should be fostered by the key account manager, who is both the sponsor and coach of the team.

Teams also need to develop their own framework for activities such as problem resolution and idea generation, developing the account plan, time management and cost management.

Senior management must create a big game atmosphere in which key account teams can see that their efforts really matter. This will be reinforced by frequent feedback on team performance and the distribution of rewards associated with team achievement.

Like all other team activity, objectives and success criteria will be necessary. Common critical success factors of key account teams might be:

- contact with customers for all members of the team – customer visits, social events etc.;
- monthly targets, however small;
- monitoring/measurement/feedback and reward;
- balance of skills appropriate to the customer's requirements;
- spirit of mutual encouragement;
- open consideration of strategic as well as tactical issues;
- leadership by key account manager.

At the synergistic stage of key account management, the key account manager and all members of the key account team will be involved in cross-boundary process teams. Working with people from the customer's organization will have even more developmental value and introduce new skill challenges such as boundary spanning. In these cases, the teams take members beyond key account skills to cross-boundary value management skills.

Conclusion

This chapter has explained how the skills needed in a key account manager evolve as the relationship between the selling company and buying company evolve, and what that ultimately means in terms of defining the top echelon of this profession. In addition, that skills portfolio has implication for the manner and level of reward and status key account managers will expect. Key account management skills also have to be developed throughout the selling company if it wants to achieve the highest levels of customer focus. Establishing and supporting key account teams will facilitate the spread of these critical competences.

Chapter 7

Positioning key account activity

Introduction

The purpose of this chapter is to discuss the positioning of key account activity in organizations. It looks first of all at how companies used to organize themselves, and contrasts them with modern interpretations of the customer-focused organization, and matrix management. The global challenge is then presented, followed by a description of current practice in the organization of key account teams. Finally, a brief future scenario is considered.

Key account management can be a considerable challenge for relatively small companies where sales, service, delivery, manufacturing and accounting departments may all have different views about any individual customer. As the scope of the company broadens, especially geographically, the scale of the key account management challenge becomes ever more complex.

Understandably, company directors ask 'how should we manage ourselves to achieve key account management?' This is a question which can only be answered in shades of grey at the moment. We can look at forms of organization which have been common in the past and note why they are not appropriate today. For today, we know that some sort of customer-focused organization is right, but there is more than one way to organize to achieve that focus. In most cases, a customer-focused organization is not sufficient in itself to ensure that the company thrives, and matrix management is becoming increasingly common.

Historical precedents

In the beginning it was simple. Sales representatives had geographical territories, probably including some customers who ordered in large volumes and lots of customers who ordered in small volumes. The sales manager was god in his or her region. The regional sales manager reported to a sales director who reported to a managing director (Figure 7.1). Sales initiatives were driven by new product lines.

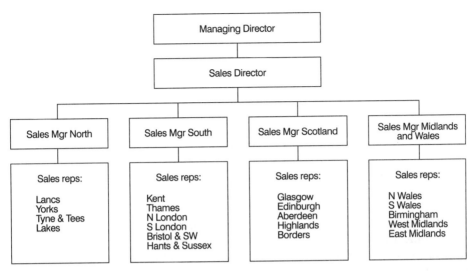

Figure 7.1 An early organizational chart

The limitations of this model were tested in the 1970s, when retailing, among other businesses became dominated by national strategy and decision making. Companies selling to national customers assigned senior sales representatives to look after the largest. Organizationally, a few selling companies changed. Some far-sighted brand leaders replaced their geographical organizations with customer-focused organizations. However, elements of the geographical branch systems usually prevailed. Figure 7.2 shows a revised organizational chart.

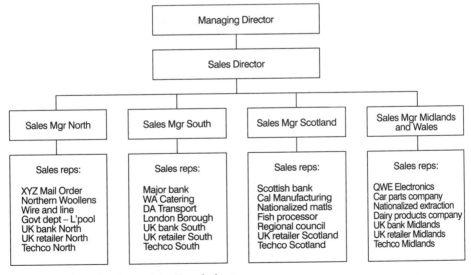

Figure 7.2 A revised organizational chart

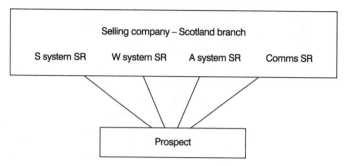

Figure 7.3 Product specialism

In the 1980s there was diversity in sales organizations. Many continued to be geographically oriented, national companies might serve customers on a national scale. However, within this apparent nationwide service, product specialists had begun to assume importance. So a customer could be faced with a collection of product sales representatives, some of whom might even be promoting competitive offerings (Figure 7.3).

Product specialism may work where there are specialist buyers. For example in large retailers, each buyer manages a specific consumer good category such as bakery, dairy, household cleaning materials, etc. For companies in which the operational managers are buying decision makers, to be faced by several product specific sales representatives from the same company is confusing and irritating. The matrix shown in Figure 7.4 illustrates this point – if there is no

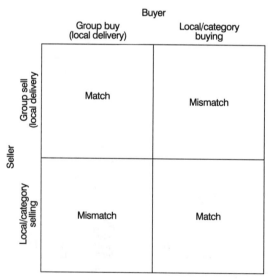

Figure 7.4 Organizational fit to meet buying company requirements

organizational fit to meet the buyer's requirements, the selling company will be introducing an element of 'hassle' for the prospect/customer which may persuade them to look for alternative sources.

We have discussed key account management as the alternative to geographical or product focus. A number of models have been observed in recent years.

Reporting lines within companies

The traditional view of the key account reporting line would assume that key account managers would report into sales and marketing, perhaps via a regional hierarchy as shown in Figure 7.5.

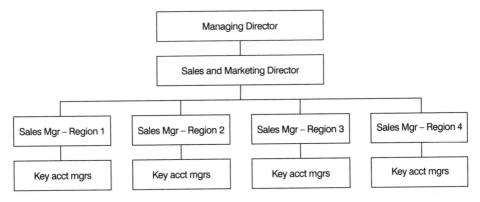

Figure 7.5 A traditional regional hierarchy

The sales and marketing director would also be expected to be responsible for brand management, marketing planning and general business development. Brand management is not as dominant in industry-to-industry markets as in consumer markets. Nevertheless, the question arises – what is the relative importance of key account managers and brand managers?

In the traditional hierarchy, when key account management was emerging from key account selling, there was an extra layer of management (the regional sales manager) which suggested that key account managers had a lower status.

It is now unusual for there to be more than one step between key account managers and general management. Recently, delayering has resulted in some dramatic variations in reporting lines for key account managers. A high proportion of companies have key account managers reporting directly to the general manager/managing director (Figure 7.6).

It is not unreasonable for a member of staff who is responsible for a strategic proportion of company turnover to have direct access to the managing director. This particular delayering has sometimes been driven by general managers having recognized a need to be in direct contact with the key account managers and the key accounts.

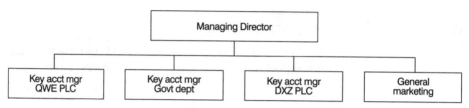

Figure 7.6 A revised hierarchy

It has also been driven by the need of customers to see that their key account manager has high status within his or her own organization. Customer decision makers are frustrated when key account managers are not empowered to make decisions. That lack of authority can usually be attributed to company hierarchies; and because of low status, the people appointed to manage key accounts have clearly not been developed to the level of professionalism required.

The reporting line of the key account manager says a lot to the buying company about their status, and will affect the seniority of the key account manager's contacts in their organization. Ideally, the key account manager should have a main contact who is a director, whether he or she is a purchasing director or an operational director, and regular contact with other senior management. In order to achieve this level of access, the key account manager will be expected to be in regular contact with his or her own board members (and have the skills and professionalism commensurate with that).

Matrix management

As if all that was not complicated enough, most companies need to achieve success on more than one organizational axis (Figure 7.7).

The shading indicates the amount of business that each division does with each customer, with black signifying that the customer uses the company for 100 per cent of a product type and white indicating that the customer does not use the company at all for that product type. While it is the role of the key account manager to turn the matrix ever darker in all applicable boxes, it may also be applicable for product managers to be ensuring that the company's

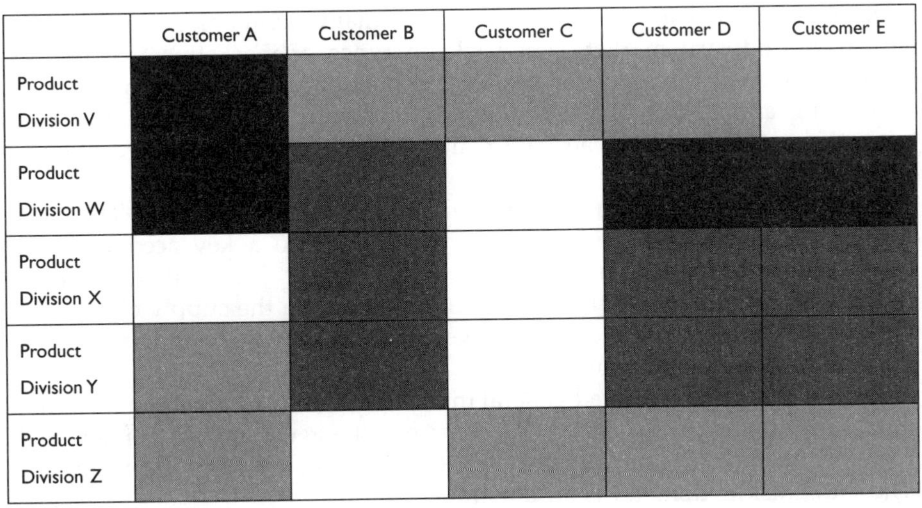

	Customer A	Customer B	Customer C	Customer D	Customer E
Product Division V					
Product Division W					
Product Division X					
Product Division Y					
Product Division Z					

Figure 7.7 Matrix management

products are ahead of the competition in terms of functionality and being made to the highest standards.

Matrix management requires the highest standards of communications and objectivity from everyone within the organization. Assuming a sufficiently large organization, there might be one manager for each product-for-account box, reporting to a divisional manager and the key account manager. In fact, if we add the third dimension of geography/culture, there might be one manager per product/customer/region cube.

Companies who are developing matrix management tend to keep the emphasis on the unit managers as members of the key account team. Their product-oriented or region-oriented role may be the subject of some objectives, but conflicts are usually resolved in favour of key account activity.

The interrelationship of key account management with general marketing

Most companies who are key account focused assign equal or greater status to key account managers than the status enjoyed by product or brand managers.

While some buying companies appreciate strong branding and merchandising in business-to-business marketing, the relationship of the key account manager with key purchasing decision makers is considered much more important. Buying companies value the support that communications or product development might make overall, but expect a great deal of tailoring of the selling company's offering to meet their particular needs.

During the recession of the early 1990s, many companies, especially in industry-to-industry markets, cut back on types of marketing expenditure where effectiveness could not be easily measured. Spending on general advertising and exhibitions was reduced in favour of promotional activity (often the attention of a key account manager) targeted at particular customers or prospects.

The shift in expenditure was bound to mean a shift in status too. The value of a selling company's general marketing activity to a key account is the knowledge, information and expertise which might enable them to work together on promotions to the next set of customers in the supply chain. Joint marketing is just one of the things a key account manager might be able to facilitate for the buying company.

This in turn has encouraged general marketing to move from a concentration on tactical campaigns to strategy delivery, e.g. the generation of demand pull from consumers to encourage customers to prefer the company and its brands. (The 'Intel inside' demand is an illustration of this.)

The global/local challenge for key account management

> 'Recruit people from all the countries you operate in, connect them to each other, move them around regularly and in thirty years' time you will have built a truly international management group.'
>
> Schlumberger, US/French oil company,
> quoted in *Global Warming* by Hall and Poots.

Achieving global scope in the organization of key account activity is the ultimate challenge, the Olympics for key account strategists.

During the 1970s and 1980s, companies who had migrated from exporting to establishing subsidiaries in overseas markets in the 1950s and 1960s were becoming complex 'multinationals'. Towards the end of the 1980s, these companies, doing business in many countries, recognized that they had replicated the old geographical fiefdoms on a larger scale, and in many cases they had also created a product or service specific focus which meant a variety of sales representatives serving one customer within a geographical territory (Figure 7.8).

The challenge was to seek global synergy, which meant that it was not necessarily effective to have country general managers operating culturally unique variations of the company. Global branding, which is attractive to companies in some industry sectors, requires global values.

In the 1990s, the business community regards the nation state as less relevant. Even the largest national markets are too small when the global economy is driven by the technology of nanosecond transfer rates for data, image and

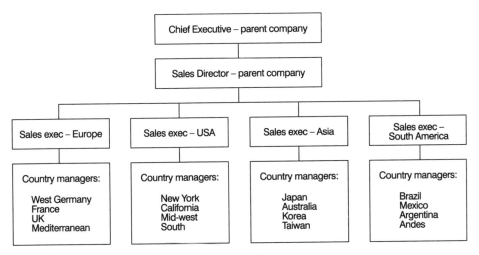

Figure 7.8 Organization of geographic territories

voice communications. The concept of 'nations = markets' emerged only in the nineteenth century and it is no longer relevant in many industry sectors. Global brands have been established, such as Coca-Cola, Sony and Guinness. Transport and communications costs have been drastically reduced and many tariffs and other barriers to international trade have been removed. Most types of manufacturing can be done anywhere in the world. 'Globalization' has to be the way forward for the ambitious large company.

There are a number of advantages to the selling company and buying company who can deal with each other on a global basis, such as consistency in worldwide standards of service, economies of scale and cultural synergy. The challenge they have is how to organize the vastness of this type of partnership. Up to 100 people in a selling company could be directly involved in managing business with a particular global buying company, talking different languages, and working in different business cultures.

Cross-cultural management is the most difficult thing that most business-people might ever do. Multinationals used to be either a collection of national companies which just happened to be commonly owned by one of those national companies, or they were dominated by the culture of the country in which the parent company was based. Full implementations of dynamic multicultural organizations are few in number and most have not been established for long enough to be assumed as successful formulae. Finding organizational structures which meet global criteria is still in the experimental stages.

Most companies on the globalization trail take one step at a time. One organizational model is frequently encountered in the initial stages of globalization (Figure 7.9).

The selling company's head office defines its global capabilities, but the global framework for each key account is negotiated in the buying company's

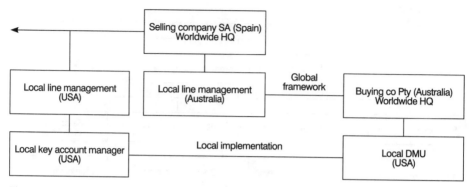

Figure 7.9 Global key account management: initiation model

'home' country. Agreements within that framework, but tailored for local conditions, are managed in each geographic market.

This model is clearly a convenient first step from multinational to global organization to meet the needs of key accounts.

This approach lays responsibility for a global account with the national subsidiary in the country of the buying company's headquarters. So, a Spanish company requires its Australian subsidiary to manage the global partnership framework for an Australian-owned worldwide company. Local delivery is managed by negotiation between the key account manager in the Spanish company's US subsidiary and the purchasing professional in the US unit of the Australian company. This style of global account management is perceived to have advantages because the selling company is always addressing buying companies within their own business culture.

An ambitious further step, of which there are a few examples, is much more purist in its emphasis on global organization (Figure 7.10).

Figure 7.10 Global key account management: line responsibility oriented to key accounts

There are further steps, although selling companies are only too aware that purer models of global key account management present considerable management challenges.

In this model, local account managers for a buying company are directly responsible to the global account manager for that buying company. They have only dotted line responsibility to local management. This model has been implemented by some leading global companies in service sectors. It represents a very strong customer focus, but in fact it may not match buying companies' organizational requirements (e.g. an in-country escalation route). It also requires all global key account managers to have cross-cultural management skills. With this model, a steering committee appears to be desirable at board level, together with a key account team, and functional teams to troubleshoot implementation. There could be up to 100 people devoted to one buying company. Above all, global key account management requires close attention to co-ordination, and sensitivity to the trade-off between global integration and local flexibility (see Millman, 1996).

In truth, there are likely to be many models in the future, and perhaps no one model will become dominant. Flexibility will be required. Depending on the way that individual buying companies want to organize themselves, selling companies may have to handle more than one model at a time.

Problems arise when global selling companies and global buying companies are not organized in mutually agreeable ways. We have already referred to the mismatch that occurs between buying companies who want a corporate approach – one key account manager conducting the whole orchestra of the selling company's offerings, and selling companies who want to offer product-specific sales representatives. The opposite of this scenario can also occur. Figure 7.4 becomes an even more critical indication of seller/buyer fit.

If both seller and buyer are organized for global business, there will be potential for achieving synergy. If both buyer and seller prefer local or category selling, their organizations are also likely to be designed to match each other. However, where mismatches occur, it is much more difficult for seller and buyer to achieve partnership.

The organization of global businesses is important and glamorous, but its significance can be overplayed. In the early 1990s there were 37,000 transnational companies who controlled one-third of the world's private sector assets. Two-thirds were national or local. Another large slice of the world economy is in the public sector. The majority of the world's citizens, while they might well be touched by the Coca-Cola or Sony global brand, will be buying it from a local or at most national retail outlet. Apart from the omnipresent McDonald's and Pizza Hut, the majority of the services they consume will be bought from local companies, or provided by local or national government.

It seems likely, that in the short term, economies of global scale will force seller/buyer dyads into a league table scenario as shown in Figure 7.11.

For example, XYZ UK might have a good, long-standing relationship with a UK supplier; and if XYZ Inc wants to purchase that selling company's goods or

Premier League	Global
First Division	Regional
Second Division	National
Third Division	Local/Niche

Figure 7.11 Seller/buyer league table

services on a global basis, the UK company will be dropped in favour of a global supplier. Occasionally buying companies operate a programme of supplier development, and help small suppliers to grow with them. In most cases, that aspect of downsizing known as supplier rationalization has seen larger companies dropping the services of smaller suppliers.

Alternatively, if a UK company is a customer of XYZ UK and XYZ Inc decides to concentrate its resources on global accounts, the national account may lose services as well as status, which means it may choose to switch to a smaller supplier to whom it will be more important.

Key account management can take place at every level. For example the owner of a carpet cleaning franchise in the local/niche league will have high volume, high profit customers on whom he or she will lavish considerable attention.

Building key account teams

In addition to discussing who key account managers report to, the question is increasingly being asked – who should report to key account managers?

In most selling companies, key account managers do not have formal or informal teams, but are expected to have influence in getting things done for their customer. This means in practice that the key account manager is constantly bidding for resources. The managers of the key account managers may assert that 'they can pull in who they need' – but buying companies will perceive that if the key account manager has to beg for the expertise they need on an *ad hoc* basis, then their needs are not strategic to the selling company.

Equally, the traditional company organization, where account managers have no other leverage over colleagues other than escalation from manager to manager is not considered by buying companies to be appropriate to meeting their needs. They expect key account managers to have more authority.

In project-based business between companies, project teams usually report on a dotted line basis to the key account manager. Semi-formal account team structures are gaining popularity for general business as well. This means that while operational staff still report to functional managers, they have dotted line responsibilities to a particular key account manager for a particular key account (Figure 7.12).

Members of teams have different line managers, but meet regularly with the key account manager and the key account, and have objectives relating to customer requirements, including a percentage of time they should be devoting to their key account. There should be some elements of shared motivation and reward, and performance on that account should lead to career development and job security for team members. In most cases of 'dotted lines', operational staff are required to report to the key account manager as well as their line manager about contacts with buying companies. The key account manager must be able to plan and monitor who is talking to who at what level.

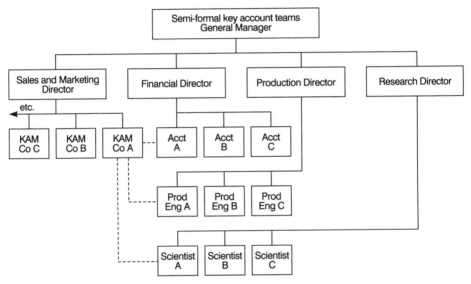

Figure 7.12 Semi-formal key account team structures

Buying companies often expect semi-formal teams to include a director as mentor. Such an arrangement adds status to the team, ensures widespread understanding of the importance of the key account focus, and improves customer perceptions.

Team members spend less time in front of the buying company than the key account manager, but they are making sure everything happens at each interface – seller/buyer relationships are multilayered and multifaceted. The key account manager conducts the orchestra. The key account manager needs to use techniques to motivate the team, such as asking one small thing at every meeting from each member that will get the company closer to the customer – e.g. redesigning a report. Meanwhile, the key account manager must also

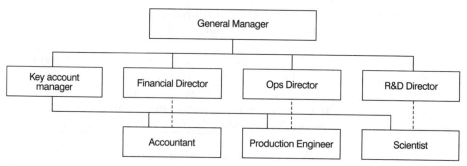

Figure 7.13 Formal key account team structures

supply lots of information to the team about the customer and its strategic objectives, and ensure that they meet their counterparts, because that encourages trust and commitment – enough for the team member to say to a line manager that an activity for that key account must take priority.

Some companies have gone further, and completely converted account managers into line managers, while functional managers have only dotted line responsibilities (Figure 7.13).

Professionals are dedicated to a particular customer and report to the key account manager. They have dotted line responsibility to functional managers.

Cross-boundary teams

Some relationships between selling companies and buying companies, where a high degree of synergy had been achieved, have regular teams working at different levels in the organization, setting their own agenda, solving their own problems with little direction from, but in communication with, the key account manager.

Considerable numbers of personnel from both the selling company and the buying company would be involved in focus teams spanning the boundary between the selling company's organization and the buying company's organization, as illustrated in Figure 7.14. The key account manager and purchasing manager work together on the partnership team and co-ordinate all other teams. The borders between selling company and buying company have become blurred. Functional and level borders are also blurred. It is the focus teams which matter because they are making things happen for the end customer. They may be issue based, project based or motivational.

There is anecdotal evidence of the members of such cross-boundary teams actually swapping jobs, from selling company to buying company and vice versa for short periods of time.

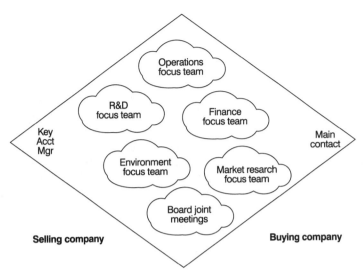

Figure 7.14 Cross-boundary teams

A key factor in achieving synergy in seller/buyer relationships is the degree to which the business processes of the two companies can be integrated.

Many seller/buyer relationships, even where there is a key account manager, are marred by disputes about inaccurate order fulfilment, invoices, and other flaws in logistics and administration. It is where companies have worked together to resolve 'hassle factors' that loyalty has built up to a degree which means the relationship might be expected to be long term.

A typical formula would be a manageably small number of joint project teams working continuously to improve specific aspects of the partnership. Besides the partnership team, which involves the key account manager, relevant operations managers and the purchasing decision makers in the buying company, there should also be a chief executive level review group and a few other focus teams involving people working at operational levels in both companies. These teams should be focused on particular interfaces between the two organizations, such as accounting transactions, stock transfer, etc.

Processes between the two companies need to be mapped, so that the partnership team involving the key account manager and his or her main contact can recommend to the board team where costs can be reduced or quality improvements might be achieved via a focus team.

In a synergistic seller/buyer relationship, the partnership performance index might comprise of 40–200 measures, which leaves plenty of scope for focus team activity. Some importance might be placed on short-term focus projects, so that personnel acquire experience of different issues and teams, and thus team tribalism and role ambiguity is avoided.

Cross-boundary teams can produce dramatic results for both selling companies and buying companies involved. Together, they can tackle higher risk activities more successfully than before, improve processes, trial new products and improve financial performance.

Both companies in such synergistic dyads also note improvements in the involvement of staff in solving problems, their understanding of each other's company and roles, and more willingness to take responsibility for getting things done. Mutual loyalty has been fostered. Measurement has provided the necessary feedback to ensure quality which both parties can be proud of.

The challenge of cross-boundary teams is to keep up the momentum. Putting teams in place causes expectations to rise, which can make it more difficult for the team to feel that it is achieving. Sometimes, one or both parties face resource constraints, such as releasing people to take part in the teams and to see through some of the team's suggestions.

Future organizational structures

As discussed further in the next chapter, the future of key account management is likely to incorporate joint value management with purchasing professionals and other key account professionals, throughout the value chain. The focus of teams and job swapping will switch from dyadic relationships to multiple relationships from raw materials processor to end-consumer.

A potential organization scenario is shown in Figure 7.15.

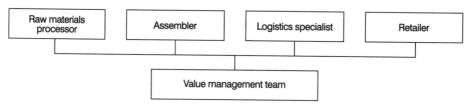

Figure 7.15 A potential organizational scenario

Conclusion

There is no set formula for the positioning of key account activity. The challenge of organizing key account management structures needs to be governed by a few critical success factors:

● Successful key account strategists counsel the avoidance of feudal and tribal sentiment in customer-facing teams, and therefore the emphasis of organization at macro and micro levels is on encouraging diversity – cross-cultural management, matrix management, multidisciplinary teams, cross-boundary teams, job swapping, etc.

- There must also be a balance between the need for consistency and stability, which is recognized by key account practitioners and the decision makers in the key account, and the flexibility which ensures dynamism in the relationship.
- Mismatches with the customer's organizational pattern and their expectations of the supplier's organizational make-up must also be avoided. It can be assumed that a variety of approaches will have to be managed.
- Whatever organizational problems occur, it must always be understood that they are irrelevant to decision makers in key accounts. The key account manager must have the authority to arrange a 'step-out', transparent to the key account.
- Whoever he or she reports to, or has reporting to him or her, the key account manager must be perceived to the customer and within the selling company as having authority, as well as being accountable. Usually buying companies complain that key account managers seem to be accountable for problems without having the authority to solve them.
- Today's organization of the key account activity must be formed with a view to the future, when co-operative value management throughout the supply chain may be the norm. Steps towards the lowering of barriers in the supply chain are all important. These usually start with multidisciplinary key account teams in the selling company and progress to cross-boundary teams involving selling company and buying company personnel.

Chapter 8

The future of key account management

The future evolution of key account management

Organizations wanting to utilize a key account management approach, will want to be assured of its future, and need to speculate what the future of key account management will be like. Having completed a thorough audit of key account management in the present, what can we predict about its characteristics in the years to come?

There are a number of possible futures for key account management, but the driving force is likely to come from customers. What happens to the concept of partnership sourcing will determine how far key account management can develop. There is a number of factors in the business environment which suggest that partnership sourcing may become more prevalent, in which case buying companies will demand high standards of key account management from suppliers. In fact, in years to come, both purchasing and marketing professionals may well be working together within companies as well as across company boundaries, looking at the entire flow from raw materials to the end

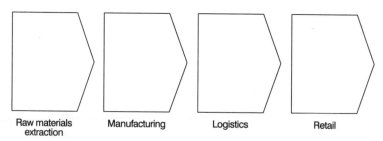

Raw materials   Manufacturing   Logistics   Retail
extraction

Figure 8.1 The linear value chain

consumer and how it can be optimized. This concept is called value management. It blows apart our view of a linear supply chain (Figure 8.1). The transfer of value will start to look more like a collection of interlocking circles (Figure 8.2), and eventually evolve into a holistic model (Figure 8.3).

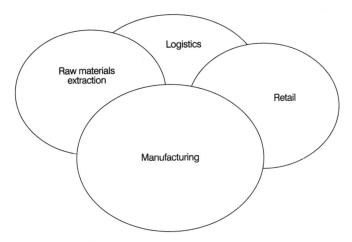

Figure 8.2 The transitional value chain

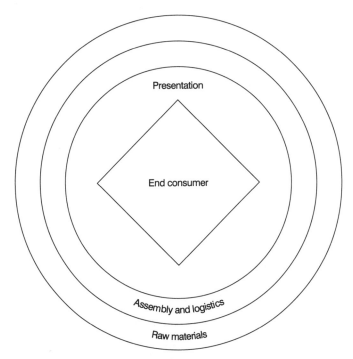

Figure 8.3 The future? Value layering

There is also an underlying assumption that the internal value chain of commercial organization will have transmuted from a linear, functional design (Figure 8.4) to a 'holistic' design (Figure 8.5).

Within this holistic model, companies will train purchasing, logistics and marketing professionals together, ensuring a consistent and integrated approach to the development of value. Job swaps within the company and across the blurred, overlapped boundaries with other companies in the supply chain, will be encouraged.

However, the belief that companies can best satisfy their customers by being tough on suppliers will not be completely eclipsed. Some business analysts

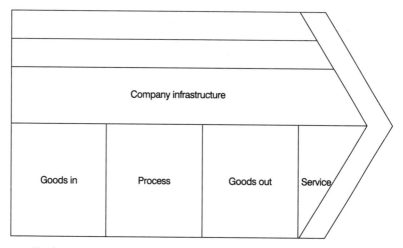

Figure 8.4 Traditional internal value chain

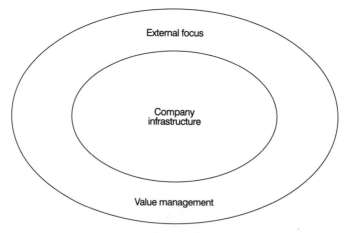

Figure 8.5 The internal value 'cake' of the future

claim that US and British business culture is adversarial, and there is not enough trust between organizations and individuals within them to make partnerships work. Just one high profile disaster involving a company operating a single sourcing policy being driven out of business by an interruption in supply would stem and reverse the trend towards partnerships. It has not yet happened. Given that most partnerships involve global-scale sellers and buyers, or a paternalistic relationship with smaller suppliers, it seems unlikely that such a disaster would occur. It may also be true that buying companies who adopt single sourcing have very robust contingency plans in the event of that single source of supply being wiped out for any reason.

Adversarial purchasing does not necessarily preclude the improvement of key account management practice, but it isolates value management on one side of the seller/buyer dyad. Change might only come if buying companies strategically decide to cut the association in the purchasing professional's mind between achieving short-term gain and career progression, mirroring what happens when selling companies develop sales representatives into key account managers. Currently, professional purchasing is still largely regarded as a matter of negotiating skill, not cross-boundary process redesign. The stereotypical purchasing manager is as rough and tough as the stereotype of a sales representative. If sales and purchasing are both to evolve into analytical and consultative roles, where will the impetus to drive supply chain dynamics come from?

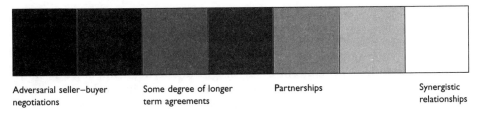

| Adversarial seller–buyer negotiations | Some degree of longer term agreements | Partnerships | Synergistic relationships |

Figure 8.6

The most likely scenario based on the findings of the Cranfield research, is that there will be a polarization in value management practice in the twenty-first century (see Figure 8.6). At one end of the spectrum, the big league global selling/buying dyads will be pursuing the leanest supply, achieving synergy and integration. This will be so especially where the value chain includes a manufacturing process. Integration will probably include cross-ownership of shares. Where power, risk and trust is in balance between seller and buyer, partnerships of equals will be highly successful. Nevertheless, there will be potential for stagnation and complacency in those partnerships. The need to market test and/or benchmark performance may be driven by third parties – professional institutions, the end-consumer, or competition legislation.

Larger companies may also emulate the Japanese model of 'benevolence through loyalty' to develop smaller suppliers. It seems likely that such arrangements may remain local and involve non-critical supplies or services. Where a smaller supplier is responsible for core products or services, the likelihood of virtual if not actual acquisition of the smaller company by the larger company is high.

At the other end of the spectrum, smaller players in smaller economies, who may not be attractive or 'key' accounts to any of their suppliers, may be forced to adopt tactical approaches to supply chain issues in order to survive.

In the middle there will be moderate degrees of preferment, including longer term contracts, accompanied by some nervousness over single sourcing and/or over-reliance on a few customers.

We have discussed in Chapter 7 the emergence of different leagues of commercial players in the private sector (Figure 8.7).

Premier League	Global
First Division	Regional
Second Division	National
Third Division	Local/Niche

Figure 8.7 Seller/buyer league table

We know that global businesses represent about one-third of the private sector worldwide. The concentration of global buying companies seeking global selling companies to ensure consistency of supply worldwide means that it will be increasingly difficult for geographically restricted players to move up to the Premier League, except via the minor element of 'benevolence through loyalty' in the system. That minor element could be critical to companies vying for promotion. The cost reductions which can be achieved through partnership would make the company more competitive and therefore better equipped to expand to a larger geographical scale.

End consumers will still perceive variety and choice in the economy, and most will still be highly dependent on local and national companies for a high proportion of their weekly spend. The role of public services may be blurred by the use of private firms to deliver those services to the end consumer, but this is most likely to provide more opportunities for local and national firms. Global economies of scale are attractive in many industry segments, but global firms will not dominate every segment.

The challenge of managing value in the supply chain will be increasingly complex. While a variety of approaches will still be observed, the partnership model will show the most significant growth trend, enabling the evolution of key account management into value management.

A mission for key account management?

A professional association for key account managers would probably have the mission to establish and maintain key account management as the dominant approach used by selling companies for building relationships with their strategic customers. It would probably also want to make key account management the profession of choice for top graduates.

In fact, this is probably not ambitious or far-sighted enough. Within the early decades of the 21st century, the concepts of key account management and supplier development will have merged into 'value management'. In the most innovative supply chains, that may happen sooner. The mission of key account management should be to transcend itself, because the boundary between selling company and buying company is becoming ever more blurred. The future dynamics of value management could be promoted in a way to ensure that top graduates would be excited by the career it can offer.

The role and contribution of key account management within firms ·

Inevitably, the role of value management in the future, as key account management is now, will be to deliver profit. Value management represents the opposite of commoditization. Commoditization is the ally of adversarial negotiation which erodes value in pursuit of low price. Key account management is today's strategy for companies who want to differentiate their product and service by value added elements tailored to each strategic customer. For example one supplier of a commodity raw material to a process manufacturer secured a partnership deal with that company by offering a consignment stock arrangement before any of its rivals. The purpose of key account management is to keep customers and achieve profit through mutual cost reduction. It is the discipline of enhancing value through better people, products, processes and communications, and will in due course be recognized and titled as such.

What customer needs does key account management satisfy?

Key account management must continue to fulfil practical customer needs. Buying companies expect that a key account management approach, as opposed to key account selling, is more than just a single point of contact. It must deliver process improvement and access to the selling company's latest technology and best people. Key account management must also fulfil the customer's intangible need to feel special. The key account must be known and welcomed by everyone in the selling company from the managing director to the cleaner.

Can key account management continue to provide distinctive competitive advantage?

It is easy to slip into the comfort zone of assuming key account management is distinctly better because it is morally and intellectually superior to seek high levels of professionalism in relationships with strategic customers! In truth, key account management is pursued because when it is done well it is a distinctive competence which leads to profit. That profit is derived firstly from the cost advantages associated with retaining customers rather than experiencing high levels of customer 'churn'. Thereafter, further profit opportunities are represented by gaining share in established accounts and process improvements identified in partnership with them. Like any profit, it is preceded by investment, the most significant of which is the training and development of the key account manager.

In the future, it will be ever more difficult to keep a 'value' edge in terms of quantifiable benefits, or even in terms of professionalism. Wider aspects of value will need to be explored. The focus may switch to supply chain ethics.

Indications for the future – where is key account management going?

Indications are that key account management and even better key account management will become a critical success factor for industry-to-industry marketing in the near future. It won't suit every supplier and every customer, but it will certainly be dominant in premier league global corporations. Eventually key account management will be transcended by value management, but the first step is to distinguish key account management from key account selling. Key account management will be perceived as best practice in selling companies, but its definition will still be evolving.

Marketing and purchasing professionals will have to work more closely together within companies as well as across company boundaries in order to improve supply flow which matches the end-consumers' demands. Eventually, the distinction between key account manager and purchasing professional becomes blurred into value managers.

It is possible that some firms, such as retailers, will never move away from adversarial purchasing, although they may well make functional improvements, such as electronic data interchange (EDI). While EDI can reduce costs dramatically, it is data, not proprietary information. A variety of relationships between selling companies and buying companies will survive into the future, but elements of wider value will be incorporated even into adversarial deals.

Summary – a mission for key account management

Figure 8.8 provides a summary of the mission for key account management.

Role	Needs fulfilled
Profit through partnership	Practical needs Need to feel special
Distinctiveness Quantifiable benefits Professionalism Ethics?	**Future** Value management

Figure 8.8 Summary – a mission for key account management

The business environment for key account management

We can be confident about the long-term future for key account management, evolving into value management, because there are a number of external drivers in the business environment.

Business folklore says that harsh cost-driven trends will be followed by people-oriented philosophies. After the recession of the early 1990s, and an era of ruthless downsizing, the time is right for a return to more positive approaches.

Politics

The stakeholder concept

The 'stakeholder concept' has recently become very popular with British politicians. In fact, it has US parentage. Decades ago, IBM inculcated the stakeholder model into its trainees. IBM's concept was that the company was responsible to a number of stakeholders:

- stockholders (shareholders);
- customers;
- employees;
- suppliers;
- community.

Delivering shareholder value was indeed supremely important, but it was necessary to do that by partnerships with customers, employees, suppliers and the community.

It could be argued that when in the 1980s IBM set itself the overriding goal of becoming the lowest cost producer in the information systems industry, the stakeholder concept collapsed and with it IBM's shareholders' value. It could also be argued, cynically, that the stakeholder model was convenient for IBM only so long as the company's huge market share made it a target for political criticism. Nevertheless, it was an interesting philosophical stance in a time when producer interests (including IBM's) were dominant in supply chains. In the 1970s, if a buying company failed to pay on time, selling companies were often powerful enough to stop their supply without notice.

The stakeholder concept has always had some elements of political support in Europe, such as employee consultation in Germany. It is perceived to be a worthy concept, which is difficult to attack, although politicians may argue about what it really means. All political parties in the UK have exhorted businesses to be more partnership oriented, but differ on whether legislation is needed on individual issues such as respecting payment terms. The alternative to punitive persuasion is financial incentive, and accountants may find that within the near future there are tax incentives for elements of partnership which will make long-term arrangements with suppliers irresistible.

Many politicians and senior civil servants believe that adversarial relationships between selling and buying companies are bad for competitiveness. For example the adversarial culture in the UK construction industry between architects, contractors and sub-contractors is believed to add 30 per cent to costs. Common sense dictates that the interests of all parties in a project are legitimate. Unprofitable suppliers are risky and unprofitable customers are also very risky. Therefore, key account management and partnership sourcing are encouraged by expert opinion.

Employment legislation

In the USA, buyers have been put under legal as well as moral pressure not to buy from suppliers who violate US labour laws, whether they are based in the USA, or other countries such as Latin America or Asia. A fifty-year-old law holds buyers liable for suppliers' illegal labour practices. Recent raids in California revealed Thai refugees in barbed wire encampments producing goods for major department stores. It is not uncommon in the USA for the law to require companies to police their sources of supply, even when those sources are outside US borders. This has always been rigidly observed in the case of regulations on food and drug production, or trading with suppliers in countries deemed to be enemies of the USA. The resurrection of this law on labour practices is merely an extension.

Consumer protection legislation

Quality and traceability have been driving forces for partnerships in manu-facturing industry. It is certain that consumer protection legislation will force the traceability issue wider and wider. For example the BSE crisis ('mad cow' disease) means that farmers expect that within a short period of time, food items will have to be traceable from the supermarket shelf to the original breeder or grower (and the parent animal). In the long run, the idea of anonymity of buyer or seller is doomed in all legitimate trade. Co-operation in the supply chain will have legislative imperatives.

Economy

Global leadership

An increasing number of world opinion leaders in business come from the Far East. These new giants are mostly manufacturing companies, whose distinctive competence is making things smaller, cheaper, faster and more reliable. Partnership between buying companies and selling companies is perceived to be part of the business culture of the Far East. Japanese companies have influenced best practice around the world. Many award-winning US and European companies have adopted policies such as partnership sourcing. It is therefore easy to conclude that partnership will become a mainstream concept in global business and demand key account management responses.

Some observers of comparative business cultures explain that it is easy to implement partnership sourcing in Japan – the sense of duty of the supplier would assure the customer of the payoff from relational contracting. They oppose the tendency of Western companies to adopt partnership sourcing, arguing that US and British business cultures imply no sense of duty. Therefore companies trying to emulate the Japanese model in a Western cultural context put themselves at unnecessary risk of an interruption of supply.

The counter argument is that companies operating on a global scale need to transcend geographically narrow definitions of business culture and adopt best practice, wherever it comes from.

Global competition

According to a study by A. T. Kearney and the Manchester School of Management (Nolan, 1996), lack of measurement and failure to exploit opportunities for supply chain integration are said to be costing the UK £2.4 billion per annum. The politicians and business associations who want to improve industrial competitiveness will continue to encourage seller/buyer partnerships.

Historical precedence

To date, partnership does have a good track record. The exception might be the relationship between Rover and Honda, which came to a dramatic end when Rover's parent company sold it to BMW. The situation brought to mind the nickname Britain enjoyed during the War of the Spanish Succession – 'perfidious Albion'. Nevertheless, the majority of partnerships which have been studied are successful. Neither key account management nor partnership sourcing can preclude situations in which a business relationship runs out of steam, or is ended through changes in ownership or extraordinary market conditions. What can be said is that, on balance, selling companies and buying companies working together to deliver value tend to carry on for as long as possible, as usually they both enjoy improved performance.

Low inflation, low interest rates

When inflation was high in Western economies, companies enjoyed a comfort zone which masked inefficiency. Now, most economists are advising us to plan for low inflation, worldwide. In fact, in many sectors worldwide, prices are falling. The combination of increased competition due to globalization, deregulation and economic management by governments has ensured inflation in the 1–3 per cent band.

In such a climate, there is no room for complacency. Business can only be won by being better than competitors and taking market share off them. Product, process and people improvements are imperative. The depth of customer feedback required to achieve continuous improvement is easier within a key account management/partnership framework.

Economic integration

The timetable for the single European currency may slip, but if the members of the European Union want to reap the benefits of being a single market, then greater economic convergence will be achieved. Large companies are already forging pan-European organizational structures and looking for pan-European suppliers and customers. Such activity reflects a scenario preferred by many business planners, that the world economy in the near future will consist of a small number of trading blocs. Other companies are planning for global integration, regardless of national or supra-national political boundaries. In economic terms, the nation state is less relevant than ever. The resurgence of nationalist emotions in various parts of the world only serves to suggest that companies with global reach should be as flexible as possible in the distribution of their resources.

Social

Sophistication of consumers

The customer may have always been hailed as king, but was not always a very well-informed monarch. The king was often at the mercy of his 'subjects' (suppliers). The rising power of consumer pressure groups and the popular media have changed all that. They have wrested power from companies and vested it in the ultimate users of their products and services. End customers expect a great deal of respect, now often contractually assured in some sort of charter document. The logical extension of this consumer-driven scenario is co-operation between all organizations delivering value in the flow of supply from raw materials to consumer. The concept of adding value is significant. Consumers will soon leapfrog any links in the supply chain which they feel do not add value.

They need raw materials to be converted into what they can use, got to where they need them and presented to them for choice (Figure 8.9). Which company in the supply chain does any of these is irrelevant.

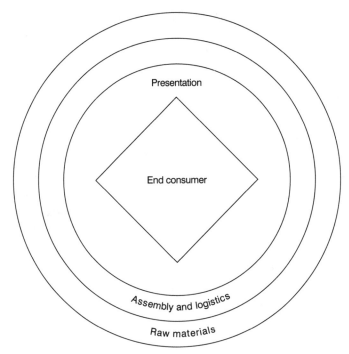

Figure 8.9 Customer focus/holistic supply

Consumer champions are casting a critical eye over the whole supply chain in the 1990s. Companies with dubious practices have been bread and butter to investigative journalists for a long time. Now, even companies with very good reputations have to be squeakier clean than ever and ensure that their values are passed up the supply chain. Marks and Spencer, usually one of the most admired companies in Europe, was recently under media fire for buying from suppliers whose suppliers were allegedly breaking local employment laws in North Africa.

So consumers may know more about supply chains than might ever have interested them ten to twenty years ago – they see it is all relevant to the end product they get. The idea of companies working together with their suppliers to deliver more value to the end consumer is an attractive one, a matter of common sense. What, after all is the opposite of a 'family' approach to the supply chain? Adversarial and promiscuous policies seem very unsophisticated, and contrary to the moral values Western as well as Eastern societies aspire to.

Ethics and the environment

Issues of ethics and the environment are gaining importance in consumer buying decisions. Partnership between different companies in the supply chain can be very environmentally advantageous. At the very least, the opportunity is usually taken to eliminate waste in supply practice. It also encourages better processes. One buying company in the Cranfield study had a problem with emissions from a particular manufacturing process. It had partnership agreements with all its key raw material suppliers, so it called them together to work with it to eliminate the emissions.

Technology

All-pervasive remote communications

People, many of whom are now in the marketing profession, are used to building relationships by telephone and electronic mail. The potential for reconfiguring supply chains and flexibility in terms of where value is perceived to be added is great. This may mean shorter supply chains or more diversity in supply chains. The effect of this can already be seen in financial services, where telephone banking and direct insurance have captured significant market share.

Information technology

The way in which sellers and buyers use information technology together will also be relevant, and is summarized in Figure 8.10.

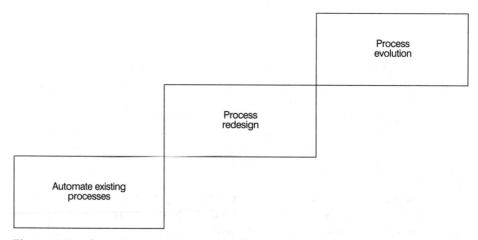

Figure 8.10 Information technology and sellers and buyers

Step 1 – Automating existing processes

Even suppliers and buyers with traditionally adversarial approaches are reaping benefits from the automation of processes between them. Technology marches ever onwards, and the potential to apply it to supply chain issues is growing. It has been claimed that electronic data interchange alone can reduce transaction costs between a selling company and their buying companies by 90 per cent.

Automating communications can also improve efficiency. Companies with global reach already rely internally and externally on e-mail communications. It overcomes time differences and the inevitable elusiveness of managers and professionals who do a lot of travelling. In some cases, business contacts have to build up relationships via e-mail.

Neither EDI nor electronic mail actually change processes, they just automate them. Many businesses are gaining advantage from going further.

Step 2 – Process redesign

Selling companies and buying companies need to move on from the use of technology to improve efficiency to the use of technology to improve effectiveness.

The prerequisite for process redesign is access to information across organizational boundaries. Without that exchange of information, no streamlining can be achieved. Seller/buyer partners are increasingly sharing common databases. The obvious example is stock management. If point of sale data is transferred to commonly held databases of stock information, suppliers of logistics services and goods can make sure that retail outlets are always fully stocked with the fastest moving lines. That way, everybody makes more money through consumers getting what they want when they want it. (Classic cases of electronic stock management include Benetton and Walmart.)

If companies in the supply chain do not learn how to share information, it could result in the reconfiguration of the chain, or its fragmentation, as manufacturers and primary service providers try to reach directly to consumers, and consumers have access to them via their home personal computers.

As companies move into implementing 'intranet' services to ensure effective access of all employees to the right quality and quantity of information, suppliers and customers could also be linked in.

Moving on from sharing information, in order to improve processes, sellers and buyers need to examine current activities together, to explore and optimize processes. There are a number of software packages which enable the modelling of supply chains and markets, and analysis of the leverage of value within them.

In order to establish opportunities for process efficiencies, it is helpful to use computer-based modelling tools to simulate flows of goods, information and value. The exploration of 'what ifs' is speedy, enabling large quantities of potential changes to be evaluated.

Politics/legislation Stakeholder concept Employment legislation Consumer protection	**Economics** Global leadership Global competition Track record of KAM/partnership Low inflation/low interest rates Integration (across national boundaries)
Social Sophistication of consumers Ethics and the environment	**Technology** All-pervasive communications Automation of processes Cross-boundary process redesign Evolutionary models

Figure 8.11 PEST analysis

Step 3 – Evolutionary benefits

Evolution, in this respect, will have been achieved when organizations can develop in ways which would not otherwise have been possible, when requirements are not clear cut. Concept modelling rather than structural modelling will be utilized – a flexible, cross-boundary technique. Concept modelling can facilitate consideration of radical options. It animates, manipulates and abstracts entities in the supply chain and removes organizational constraints. This technique is still being developed and automated by information systems specialists.

Figure 8.11 provides a summary of this section.

Customer drivers

In addition to external drivers towards partnerships between selling companies and buying companies, there are factors internal to the seller/buyer relationship. Selling companies may be pro-active in offering higher and higher standards of key account management, but it is the receptiveness of the customer that is critical in achieving great advances.

The pressures on customers to consider partnership with suppliers are not just present in the business environment. There is also an internal focus. Buying companies need to identify new routes to profit, continually improve quality, and review the nature of functions such as purchasing and how they can deliver more value.

There is growing evidence that partnership reduces costs. Up to 70 per cent of costs in a company can be associated with supply chain issues, so there is plenty of opportunity for improvement and a need to focus on smart solutions. In a 1995 survey, Partnership Sourcing Limited reported that in 75 per cent of seller/buyer partnerships, costs had been reduced, and in 70 per cent quality had improved. A number of initiatives can contribute.

Attention to detail – quality and traceability

Customers want quality through attention to detail – solving 'soft management issues'. Quality is not just about traceability and accountability. Some selling companies have hundreds of quality indicators including the time taken to answer the phone. Any customer wanting to initiate new quality indicators with a supplier is more likely to do so if there is a strong element of trust and partnership.

Smart purchasing

Senior managers in many companies are examining the role of the purchasing department in delivering the company's overall strategies. Professional purchasing needs to move on from negotiation skills to management skills, otherwise it is a prime candidate for outsourcing. Many large companies have contracted out purchasing. If all that is needed is deal makers – it is a cost-effective thing to do.

Others conduct benchmarking of their purchasing practice. Benchmarking services are available, 3200 companies are regularly examined by consultancy PIMS. They calculate that the difference between good and bad practice in purchasing is at least five per cent on the cost of goods and services.

A well-constructed, concentrated supply base can contribute to better profitability. In order to increase the level of success, the purchasing function must measure its effect on organizational costs and operational costs and compare the results with prices.

Lean supply

Managers understand that, for a product or service to be commercially advantageous to the provider – value must be added faster than cost.

Lean supply involves the study of the entire supply flow from raw materials to consumer – the concept is that it is all an integrated whole. Interfaces between companies are artificial. Therefore, the recognition of costs associated with any departure from perfect execution of tasks is necessary to provide long-term customer satisfaction. The effects of any inefficiency are not limited to a specific employer.

In theory, effective supply flow is an absolute. In practice, you just have to keep applying continuous improvement to be leaner than the competition. Adopting an approach in which supplier and customer are joint guardians of value in transit is vital to that. Examination of value in transit demands that both supplier and customer open their 'books' and facilitate two-way assessment in order to optimize performance. There should be no blame and no excuses. Lean supply practice also lends itself to sharing some costs critical to mutual success, such as R&D and training.

Lean supply has been a dominant strategy where physical parts are moved along the supply chain. An even more popular phenomenon has been the concept of facilities management of non-core services.

Extending facilities management

The concept of a supplier working on customer premises, reporting to customer managers, is common in catering, cleaning and security. These are all non-core activities which are contracted out for a fixed number of years to specialist companies. The boundaries between supplier and customer are blurred, and supplier staff can quite clearly see the 'end consumer' of their services.

Facilities management (FM) has been extended in recent years – to information systems, engineering maintenance and property management. The latest variation on FM is the call centre for customer service. Instead of in-house call-handling, companies engage call centre specialists. Their staff may either operate from the client's premises or from a remote location linked by information technology (data, voice and, increasingly, image).

FM is generally based on long-term contracts and a wide variety of performance measures. Since the supplier is working with the customer on the customer premises, seller/buyer relationships are likely to be very comprehensive.

The sum of these trends is buying company demand for key account management in the short to medium term and a high probability of a joint value management future.

What could stop the trend towards value management?

The persistence of adversarial relationships in the supply chain cannot be overlooked. Key account selling is alive and well and an appropriate response to adversarial purchasing. But it has nowhere to go. Companies faced with adversarial purchasing may have to leap over the gatekeeper and build different types of relationships with the next group of buyers. Even food manufacturers send marketing messages and samples direct to consumers by mail, and encourage them to order by telephone/Internet. As electronic communications become more widespread, it will be easier for those adding value in the supply chain to reconfigure it.

There are undoubtedly factors which can turn customers against key account management. Selling companies need to remain vigilant. Letting a customer down must be strenuously avoided, as it is fear of such let-downs which prevents many willing buying companies from making their preferred supplier their partner.

Customers are most likely to reject partnership under the following circumstances:

- *Close proximity to a single sourcing disaster*
  There may be no famous cases of a company having gone bust because of an interruption in supply from a partnership supplier, but the potential exists. In fact, problems are more likely to be caused by 'lowest tender' suppliers.
- *Perceiving an imbalance in size and power with the selling company*
  Most business professionals are familiar with Porter's analysis of competitive forces and their effect on profitability (Figure 8.12). There is an underlying assumption in this analysis that there are power struggles in the value chain. Developing trust can, over time, reduce fear of suppliers' power.
- *Perceiving that the selling company is proposing insufficient benefits*
  Customers may have high expectations which the selling company cannot meet.
- *Concern about the effects of competition law*
  Competition law may be invoked at some time in the future by selling companies who feel that they have been excluded from legitimate business by a synergistic relationship between a supplier and customer. Buying companies are wary of supporting, explicitly or implicitly, monopolistic arrangements. The solution for all parties concerned is regular and rigorous market testing of incumbent suppliers.

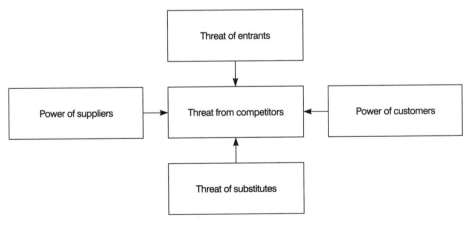

Figure 8.12 Porter's five forces analysis

- *Anticipation of future complacency*
  Some business partnerships do run out of steam. What is a buying company supposed to do when its partnership supplier has fallen behind its competitors in terms of product innovation, or employee professionalism? Civilised exit plans are required in any partnership to reassure either party that fundamental grievances can be managed.
- *Concern about boundary spanning, role ambiguity, succession*
  The more we talk about integration, the more we create ambiguity for employees. The employer no longer represents a tribal interest. Reason and co-operation is supposed to prevail. This is difficult for people who have a need for identification, and many do. Just as selling companies fear key account managers identifying more closely with a customer than their own employer, buying companies also fear purchasing professionals feeling too much for a supplier's point of view. More and more flexibility is being demanded in the workplace. Like many other human resource issues, role ambiguity has to be managed, it cannot be ignored.

  Succession problems are also likely to get bigger as more supplier and customer personnel work together, but then succession plans should also be business as usual.

In all these concerns of buying companies, selling companies might well see some of their own reservations about closer relationships in the supply chain. These concerns if anything suggest even more need for the ultimate transition to value management. A focus on value would eliminate many psychological boundaries which have become associated with organizational boundaries.

Strategies for selling companies

Selling companies that wish to establish themselves as leading edge will be taking a progression of steps into the future (Figure 8.13).

Establish clear water between professional key account management and the key account selling

The first challenge is to establish clear water between professional key account management and the key account selling of the past. There are a number of activities which support this strategic move.

Research by A. T. Kearney and the Manchester School of Management (Nolan, 1996) has indicated that the foundation stone of improving performance in relationships with customers is monitoring and measurement. Each relationship must be measured at the transactional and process level, and at the strategic level. Reference has already been made in this book to partnership agreements with over forty quantifiable items to be reviewed monthly. Other selling companies start by rigorous internal measurement. Attention to detail is a quality attitude which is universally welcomed by customers and helps to establish an aura of integrity and professionalism at all levels.

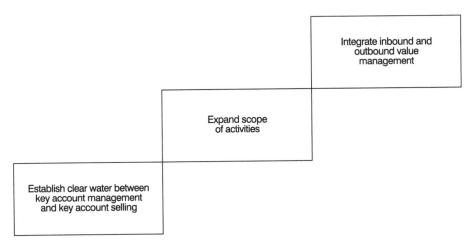

Figure 8.13 Strategies for selling companies

Related to this is continuous improvement of the product or service on which the company's identity is based. The best of professional relationships will not be able to survive a deterioration in the competitive position of the selling company's core offering. In addition to continuous improvement, it is helpful to be the initiator of dramatic breakthroughs in technology or service delivery. Buying companies like to see their chosen suppliers acquire prestige alongside discovering better ways of fulfilling their needs.

The pioneering selling company must also invest in the training and development, not just of the key account manager, but the whole customer-focused teams. This subject has been discussed at length in another chapter, but it is worth repeating that assigning multiple levels and functions of staff with objectives related to particular customers' needs will weave the philosophy of key account management into the whole fabric of the company.

One of the technical specialisms which the selling company needs to acquire is understanding of processes, whole supply chains and transfer of value. This will probably be vested in functional experts, although the key account managers will also need to know something about these topics.

Expand scope of activities
The second step is much more speculative, and will not be appropriate to every company. However, the thought processes generated by examining it will have generic value.

Computer companies in the late 1980s/early 1990s, had to migrate from promoting their proprietary systems in isolation, to providing complete solutions for customers. This meant that they had to work together with other suppliers of information systems and services on what were usually called systems integration projects. In the first instance, they had to establish tactical alliances with companies who might in other circumstances be competitors, in order to gain mutual benefit from fulfilling a customer need. In some cases, these relationships developed into strategic alliances.

All selling companies should consider how they might expand their scope of activities with customers. The customer may well require a supplier to work together with other key suppliers to solve a particular problem. Pro-actively presenting new, integrated solutions to customers would be even more attractive to them. Apart from anything else, it reduces the fear of monopoly associated with single sourcing, if the single source is, in effect, a variety of consortia (perhaps, but not necessarily, with common leadership).

The nature of solution selling has side-effects. Firstly, promotional activity is unlikely to be specific to a particular product or service. It is more likely to be about corporate identity and values. It is best delivered through seminars or other teaching-based approaches. Solution selling also leads to value-based pricing, a challenge too vast to describe here, which requires high level risk management, financial management and project management skills in both buying and selling company.

Integrate inbound and outbound value management

The last step shown in Figure 8.13 is value management. Selling companies can initiate changes in their supply chain by changing what they do with their own purchasing function. Inbound and outbound value managers ought to be singing from the same hymn-sheet. It may take some time before we see working examples of the holistic rather than the linear approach to value chains, but we can prepare for it. Working together starts with training together. Recruitment patterns for purchasing and key account management will also become similar. The two functions may switch or share roles. The potential for creating versatile value management teams is considerable.

Summary

Key account management is becoming an increasingly important profession because of dynamics in the business environment which are driving a transition from a linear to a holistic approach to external and internal value chains.

Adversarial approaches will not disappear, but may well be marginalized.

The mission for key account management will be to achieve profit through partnership by fulfilling practical customer needs, demonstrating quantifiable benefits and high professional standards.

Ultimately key account management as a profession should aspire to transpose itself, together with purchasing, into value management.

The factors in the business environment which are driving the trend towards value management include political promotion of the stakeholder concept, the influence of Far Eastern companies, consumer sophistication and the impact of communications technology.

Buying companies are being driven towards closer relationships with suppliers by the need for traceability, smart purchasing, lean supply and facilities management.

The trend towards value management could be arrested by fear factors, which selling companies need to address.

Selling companies need to step up from establishing clear water between key account management and key account selling, to expanding their scope of activities and then integrating inbound and outbound value management.

Mini-cases

Introduction

The following mini-cases are offered to readers as a way of considering just some of the complex issues which face all organizations who are serious in their intentions to build profitable and lasting relationships with customers. All companies and characters are fictional but the cases are based on real dilemmas encountered by contributors to Cranfield's key account management research. Please 'role-play' the characters in the mini-cases, but also consider what would happen in your company if it were faced with the situation described, and how you think your customer would react.

We have included a brief discussion at the end of each mini-case. We stress that these are not answers, as there is never a perfect answer to any problem in life. Please compare our thoughts with your own, and please discuss them with colleagues, as this is the best way to learn.

Case 1 – Smith and Jones Systems plc

Smith and Jones Systems plc provided a 'turnkey' information systems solution for a major government department five years ago, which they continue to support. Relationships between the board of S&J and the senior civil servants in the department are very positive. However, the key account manager absorbs most of the stress inherent in the business relationship. He has had to mediate in disagreements between S&J and government technical staff on a few occasions when the system has not met user expectations. In addition, the system now needs a major upgrade, which has been delayed because of budget constraints. The perceptions of users are that the S&J system is creaking at the seams and S&J are not responding to their needs to squeeze more out of it.

The government has now decided that it wants to contract out all the IS operations of this department, which will mean any bidder taking on all the civil service technical staff in the unit, as well as being given the challenge of upgrading the system and keeping it up to date. The opportunity will be advertised in the *European Journal* and subject to all the usual public sector tender approval procedures, designed to ensure fairness and objectivity.

As an existing supplier, Smith and Jones Systems plc are invited by the senior civil servants in the department to a meeting, to be informed of the new situation (the grapevine had already got to the key account manager). The meeting involves the managing director and the key account manager from S&J, and, from the customer, the head of department and head of IT (the latter will probably be transferred to the employment of whoever wins the bid). Officially, the department staff are only one small part of the decision-making procedure for the new contract, but they can influence the brief. Meanwhile, S&J have concerns about whether it is strategically appropriate for them to bid for an 'outsourcing' contract, and whether it can compete with the two big players in public sector outsourcing. However, it does not really want to lose this flagship customer . . .

How should they conduct the meeting?
What did they decide to do as a result of it?

S&J has clearly had problems integrating their operations with the customer's, and has not developed the network of contacts seen at the Mid-KAM stage. Consequently, it is starting at a disadvantage. Nevertheless, at the meeting, both representatives from Smith & Jones Systems plc should show real enthusiasm for the proposal and should act as if they were extremely keen to proceed with this outsourcing opportunity, and put the relationship on a new footing. The objective should be to collect as much information as possible about overheads, including salaries, terms and conditions, and details of all fixed and variable costs. Crucial to any potential bid will be a deep understanding of all the tasks undertaken by the customer's information systems department. The purpose of this is to establish whether there is likely to be sufficient margin in such a contract to warrant starting what will, in effect, be a new business venture.

Having done these calculations, the company should decide how it is going to respond to the trend towards outsourcing of information systems work. There are three options:

- ignore it, and continue to be a software house;
- form alliances with outsourcing specialists;
- diversify into outsourcing.

In order to be an outsourcing company or even an alliance partner of one, S&J would have to invest a great deal in relationship building and understanding how to manage in different company cultures.

In the event, even the 'one-off' opportunity was considered to be such a radical departure from S&J's core business, that they decided to forego the opportunity. They worked with the large consultancy that won the bid, and were eventually taken over by them.

Case 2 – Excellent Process Products

Excellent Process Products (EPP) was spun off from a large manufacturing conglomerate in 1994. The former parent, GLOSS plc, is still the dominant account in the EPP portfolio, representing 40 per cent of business.

Old loyalties are beginning to break down. The financial controller of GLOSS has recently complained to the purchasing director that he has had to allocate senior staff to spend days sorting out EPP invoices. Apart from being arithmetically inaccurate, which is just pure sloppiness, they are presented in a way which makes it very difficult for people approving the invoices to reconcile them to products which they know have been received.

The purchasing director himself is aggravated because he perceives that the new key account manager his senior buyer is dealing with is inexperienced in comparison with his predecessor, and cannot always make decisions without referral to the sales director. There is no doubt that the services of EPP are first class and good value, and he does not want to seek an alternative supplier. However, the company is making itself difficult to deal with, and he wants to take a relatively hard line to ensure that it improves.

He decided to request a one-to-one meeting with the sales director, but discovers that he is on holiday. The purchasing director is in no mood to wait, but refuses the offer made by the sales director's PA of a meeting with the key account manager. He does not say so, but he does not believe that the key account manager could initiate the changes he wants.

The sales director's PA informs the key account manager for GLOSS that the purchasing director has tried to contact the sales director. The key account manager has had little contact with the purchasing director, as his main contact is the senior buyer.

What should he do to resolve the immediate need to identify the purchasing director's concerns?

What ought to be done in the long term to improve relationships between EPP and GLOSS?

EPP has obviously made one of the cardinal mistakes in key account management. Putting a comparatively junior manager into such a pivotal key account in the mistaken belief that old loyalties will see the relationship through is irresponsible in the extreme. Major accounts must know that their business is in the hands of a senior person who can take decisions as and when necessary.

In this particular case, no doubt EPP's key account manager for GLOSS plc by now understands some of the reasons for the purchasing director's concern. His pressing task must be to reassure GLOSS, probably by getting another EPP director to visit the purchasing director immediately, so that the operational concerns may be attended to as a matter of urgency. This will at least allay fears until the return of the sales director. The more difficult issue concerning the nature of the relationship and representation issues can then be tackled by EPP. Clearly, however, the status of the key account manager for GLOSS needs to be raised.

Besides this, there is a need for involvement of more EPP staff to resolve process issues. For example a focus team of EPP sales ledger and GLOSS bought ledger staff must be set up to sort out the invoicing problems. The key account manager must ask the sales director to support him and apply pressure to other functional managers to support such initiatives. The sales director must also lobby the managing director to ensure that the key account manager has a permanent team of named functional professionals who will have some objectives placed on them related to his account. Those objectives must be set by the key account manager, so that he has authority to get things done for the customer.

(You may think that this case is far-fetched, but it is based on a real situation!)

Case 3 – All Components plc

All Components plc is a key target for Special Raw Materials Limited (SRML). Although it is not the biggest company of its type, since it has been dealing with Japanese motor companies in the UK, All Components have been looking to replicate the partnership agreements it enjoys with customers with its critical suppliers. This means that some suppliers will be assured of 100 per cent of their business for five years at a time (assuming excellent performance). All Components declaration of interest in 100 per cent partnerships has meant considerable competition among the suppliers who might be eligible.

A key account manager, Damon Riley, was assigned in April 1996, and he has worked very hard, at significant cost to SRML, to convince All Components that they would be their best partner for strategic raw materials. The effort included pilot deliveries at special prices which demonstrated the quality of SRML products. Now, eighteen months later, the big opportunity to gain 100 per cent of All Components business is on the table.

However, All Components is looking for terms and conditions which are not common in the business. For example, it wants to be able to choose its own key account team, including technicians, it wants SRML to manage the raw materials stocks on a consignment basis, and it wants up to forty success criteria to govern the ongoing relationship.

It also wants extended credit from SRML. Damon quickly assures it that consignment stock and the forty success criteria are acceptable. He tells All Components that he must take its other requests to the board. Of course, the board will be expecting him to make a recommendation.

What will Damon's recommendation be?

SRML takes equal opportunities very seriously, and the board would be worried about allowing a customer to choose its own key account team. While accepting that a good personality fit is important, normally team members would be chosen by SRML on the basis of their career development, not a customer's preference. Changes would only be made if a team member made a mistake which caused serious customer discontent.

SRML is also reluctant to extend more than thirty days' credit, even to the most strategic of customers, due to effect on cash flow and the cost of working capital.

Damon recommends to the board that:

SRML offer All Components a team somewhat more highly skilled and experienced than the account might expect. Its request to choose the team might well come from insecurity, and the offer of a top team should diffuse it. If the team is introduced to its opposite numbers by an SRML director at a social event, this will be an opportunity to build up mutual liking and respect with its opposite numbers, and will show high level endorsement of the people chosen for the account.

On the credit issue, SRML could hide behind proposed UK legislation to ensure prompt payment, although the partnership is also likely to operate in countries where extended credit is not only legal, but business as usual. An alternative would be to make an exception, provided interest were paid. Nevertheless, since the volume of business which could flow from the partnership is substantial, All Components would doubtless be disappointed with such a compromise. Damon recommends that 60 days' credit is formally agreed with them for an initial twelve-month period. SRML should reserve the right in future years to vary credit terms in line with exceptional economic conditions or local legislation.

He also recommends that, assuming his recommendations are acceptable to the board and to the prospect, that board members become involved in the formal signing of the partnership agreement with directors of All Components. Assuming it is agreeable to both companies, the trade press could be invited. Both companies would gain favourable publicity for their flexible, partnership approach.

Case 4 – Punch Financial Services

Jo Young, who works for Punch Financial Services is key account manager for Clover plc, an innovative fertilizer company. Punch is well known for its co-ordinated approach to customers' risk management – key account teams consist of a variety of specialist underwriters.

She is approached by Brian Dale, the borough finance officer of a very large London local authority. He has heard about Punch, and Jo herself, from someone he knows at the golf club who was at university with her. His authority has a myriad of suppliers of financial services, and he would like to start consolidating with fewer suppliers as contracts come up for renewal. Because of public procurement procedures, he cannot promise a full partnership, and he makes it clear to Jo that Punch must compete with incumbent suppliers on price.

Jo listens politely, thanks the borough finance officer for his interest, and says she will come back to him to suggest how they might proceed.

Punch operates very proactive prospect targeting, and one of the key criteria used is that companies of strategic interest to Punch are likely to be in high risk businesses. Punch has never done any work in central or local government. Although the company has never turned 'bluebird' business away in the past, Jo is not entirely sure that it would do either party any good to do business on a transactional basis. The borough council would never be 'key' to Punch, whereas it might be 'key' to another financial services company.

Then she considers that the nature of government in the UK has changed significantly over the 1980s and 1990s, and there are new opportunities for shared risk. Perhaps Punch ought to rethink its aversion to public sector business?

What does she decide to do?

It is always very flattering to know that a contact has recommended you to another organization, and instinctively we want to do a good job for the person who is approaching you on this basis. Jo could treat this as a test case, to explore whether opportunities really do exist for building some kind of profitable partnership with local authorities.

However, difficult choices do have to be made in key account management. Punch cannot afford to be all things to all people, and must be pragmatic. This London local authority is likely to be in the bottom right-hand box of Punch's account portfolio matrix. The reason is that the profit opportunities are likely to be minimal, and Punch's strengths compared to others are also likely to be minimal. While Jo might indeed want to do a good job for Brian Dale, he is working in a political environment where his professional judgement could be overruled. Learning the formal and informal decision-making structure of a big local authority would be a major challenge.

Jo decides to supply the minimum information necessary to ensure Punch is included on the tender list. If invited to tender, she would submit a standard proposal, but would make no allowances for Brian's warnings on price. In fact, she would probably have to include a substantial contingency to compensate for the risk to Punch of taking on non-core business. This means that she keeps faith with Brian and the contact who recommended her, while also keeping faith with Punch. In the unlikely event of the tender being successful, the business would be treated as incremental and transactional, a one-off. It could generate useful cash for Punch, without having to tie up too many scarce resources chasing low margin business. Punch has a special department to look after tactical business.

Had an invitation to tender been received without the personal contact and apparent keenness of the finance officer, Jo would definitely have decided not to submit a proposal.

The situation would have been quite different had it been a food or chemical company (i.e. high risk). Punch would have seen an opportunity for at least a twenty-year relationship and would have invested considerable resources and effort into learning about the prospect and its risk management challenges. It would have ensured a highly competitive, value-based proposal was presented.

Case 5 – Well & West plc

The logistics division of Well & West plc (LogFast) distributes extremely high volumes of low value products for X.Market Trader (XMT) Limited. XMT is exceedingly entrepreneurial in style, which has caused one or two culture clashes with the more conservative LogFast. However, the relationship seems to thrive on the challenge, and both supplier and customer demonstrate significant commitment to each other and work very closely together. Focus teams involving personnel at all levels from both companies have been formed to examine ways in which mutual cost reduction and quality improvement can be achieved.

Well & West has a number of other divisions. One (HighShift) is the market leader in the distribution of high value goods.

XMT deals in high value products as well as low value products, although volumes of high value products are quite low. The distribution director of XMT wants to do business with HighShift on same basis as LogFast.

To date, LogFast's key account manager has been avoiding the issue, as the internal rivalry between LogFast and HighShift within Well & West is not something he particularly wants to, or is able to explain. The sales director of LogFast has been pleading with his counterpart in HighShift to join the very positive business relationship they have with XMT, but without success.

The distribution director of XMT is getting impatient, and the key account manager and sales director of LogFast know that they have to make a case to the main board of Well & West. Even if they succeed, the sales director of HighShift might be infuriated and obstructive, which might not help the customer.

What case do they make, and what happens next?

This is a fairly typical problem that customers have with their suppliers. Indeed, what emerged clearly from our research was that the customer is intolerant of internal conflict within the supplying organization, so this issue needs to be resolved quickly.

It is clear that Well & West runs the risk of losing the XMT business unless its own group's internal divisions can be resolved.

The issue has to be escalated to board level in a purely objective way. A cost/benefit analysis is required, so that no one is in any doubt how much business will be lost unless HighShift co-operates with LogFast. Furthermore, the same document should raise the general issue of how the group should deal with customers requiring one policy.

One possible solution would be the creation of a key accounts division, which can be seen as independent of the functional divisions. Of course, key account team members would still have to be drawn from other divisions. They must have objectives placed on them which relate to achievement for the key account. In practice, this often leads to the erosion of divisional 'tribal' rivalries, which delivers benefits for the customers and the company overall.

Case 6 – Workwise Uniforms

The sales director of Workwise Uniforms has just had a meetings with the key account manager for its top client and her identified successor, who announced that they were both leaving to join a top competitor.

They complained about lack of status and authority, a situation which the sales director has known about for some time, but has been unable to convince the managing director that key account managers and key account teams should be more empowered. (He also knew that the key account manager had been disappointed because the market position of her client had slipped from number one in their sector to number three, and she had wanted him to move her on to a client on the way up their league. This the managing director had also blocked because of her popularity with the company's top account.)

The irony is that Workwise Uniforms encourages empowerment, among other positive employment practices, in its clients. It would be hugely embarrassing if its competitor was able to boast about the defection of key staff because Workwise did not practice what it preached. It was the sort of story that certain business magazines might be delighted to get their hands on.

Needless to say, the sales director would also have to deal with the client. The top decision makers would be devastated to lose not only their popular key account manager, but the team member who had been presented to them as her eventual successor. It would be difficult to match someone else to their exacting requirements at short notice.

What should the sales director do next?

The sales director has two issues to address here. First, there is the immediate problem of the defection of the key account manager and her number 2. Here, the only solution would appear to be for the sales director to take on the account personally until staff can be recruited to replace them. He should also be totally honest with the client, explaining what has gone wrong and informing them that any future key account manager will be given more reassurance about their status and authority.

The second issue is, of course, the issue of empowerment generally in Workwise. It needs to establish general principles, a framework for decision making within the company. Consultation should take place with staff and key accounts to find an optimum solution which will provide all-round satisfaction.

Case 7 – Jellox SA

Ideally, Jellox SA would like to ensure that its partnership suppliers do not work with its competitors. However, since competition law precludes them being able to enforce such a demand, it has placed on its suppliers the burden of convincing them that no possible cross-fertilization can take place between what they do for Jellox and what they do for their top rival, NV plc.

How should the suppliers respond?

As has been explained, competition law in the UK and Europe states that anything offered to one customer by a supplier, must theoretically be offered to all. Key account strategy offers the opportunity to tailor products and processes so closely to an individual customer that no key account would get the same formula. They would get what offers them best value.

Most suppliers faced with this challenge from customers are careful to ensure 'Chinese walls' between key account teams. Confidentiality agreements are signed, which include the pledge that no member of the designated key account team will work in the competitor's team, even for a certain period after their duties may have changed.

Case 8 – HighRisk Products Limited

Winston James is the technical manager for HighRisk Products Limited. The company has just installed new processes and received training from ProcessMaster plc. While the new processes are still parallel running with the old, something goes terribly wrong with them. The operatives claim that they have been following ProcessMaster instructions to the letter.

The failure attracts top management attention. Winston calls in the consultant who delivered the training, who, in front of the human resources director, accuses the operatives of sabotaging the new processes because of their resistance to change. Winston, fuming, asks her to leave the premises and declares that the purchasing director will have to sort out some compensation with the key account manager while he concentrates on making sure that the customers of HighRisk Products get what they have ordered using the old processes. However, he is worried that the human resources director might just have seen some justification for the accusation of resistance to change.

A large post mortem meeting is called, involving all interested parties from HighRisk and ProcessMaster. Meanwhile, Winston works all the hours he can to keep products flowing to customers while also finding out more about the failure of the new processes. He concludes that there had been flaws in the delivery of the training, but it also seems to be the case that one or two 'opinion leaders' on the shopfloor have been fomenting discontent.

Winston knows that, whatever the outcome of the meeting with Process-Master, he has a huge problem on his hands restoring the morale and motivation of the workforce, but it is one that he feels very unwilling to admit to anyone else.

What happens at the meeting?

What DOES NOT happen is the trainer repeating her accusations, and there is no 'banging of the table' which will ensure ProcessMaster is blacklisted forever more . . .

What does happen is the key account manager of ProcessMaster has to be empowered to offer compensation and training alternatives. He needs to secure the opportunity to talk to the HighRisk workers to find out what their problems are, and try to arrange more training for them. He can probably second-guess Winston's anxiety, and needs to ensure that technical expertise is available to him full-time to offer support and make sure that he comes up smelling of roses!

The board of HighRisk Products know that it needs the new processes, and is unlikely to chuck ProcessMaster off-site, unless it is offensive. If it demonstrates appropriate humility and a genuine desire to put things right, it is likely to be given the chance to do so.

Ironically, it is often in the context of putting problems right that stronger relationships can be forged between suppliers and customers. Problem accounts have been transformed into reference accounts!

Case 9 – 234 Services (UK) Limited

John Uplook, general manager of 234 Services (UK) Limited, a market leader in office services, thinks that it has a very good record on key account management. In fact, he thinks that it is master of best practice in key account management.

One of 234's prize accounts is Telephony (UK) Limited. The managing director of Telephony (UK) Limited, Rod Lines, has appeared in 234's national magazine advertisements, praising their services. Privately, however, he is irritated by what he perceives as a cultural fault – their market leader arrogance – and a tendency to quote prices which they then lower when he challenges them.

The public closeness of 234 and Telephony has not stopped 234's nearest rival, Green and White (UK) Limited, from targeting Telephony (UK) Limited, and Rod Lines in particular. It is offering him better prices first time, without time-consuming negotiation. It displays eagerness for his business, rather than condescension, and its products are just as good. Rod feels obliged to let it pitch for his business, but he does not welcome the hassle that changing supplier would cause. He would prefer 234 to be more like Green and White in its approach. He knows that the culture of 234 comes directly down to the key account teams from the very macho general manager.

What can he do, short of changing supplier, to convince John Uplook that he ought to change?

The first action that Rod Lines should take is a thorough analysis of the value that his company receives from 234, rather than concentrating solely on price. If the same value can be achieved from Green and White at a lower price, then it is his duty to change suppliers. Before doing this, however, he should insist on a bid from both companies for a 100 per cent partnership arrangement, not to help him decide on price, but to help him decide on value.

If he really prefers to keep 234 having done this, he should have a frank meeting with 234 on the basis of total value and the nature of the desired relationship. In this case, he was reassured that they would respond to his requirements.

If, after this, he had still been unsure about 234's cultural capability to adopt a partnership approach, he would have had two options:

● switch 100 per cent to Green and White;
● manage the status quo.

Many purchasing decision makers feel the need to ensure some degree of competition for their business, because they associate risks with single sourcing, such as the complacency of the supplier.

Case 10 – XYZ Global

XYZ Global has announced to the world its plans to reduce its lines to a few global brands and to reduce its supplier base from 500,000 to 50,000. All existing suppliers have to bid for the global business. ION Services will no longer be able to serve XYZ separately in the UK, Belgium, Brazil and the USA. ION has no problem in demonstrating a presence in all the countries of the world that XYZ operates, but whether it can offer a consistent standard of service globally is quite another matter.

ION has to be a front runner for XYZ's property services, it already has a majority share by being its supplier in four out of the twenty countries in which it has major plants. Most of the competitors do not have offices in other countries, just alliances with other independents.

XYZ has given its potential suppliers three years to build up to the global bid. ION has to win. The company might not stand the shock of losing a key account in four countries at once. Apart from that, it is obvious that achieving the global co-ordination required by XYZ will stand it in good stead for winning business with other global companies.

What sort of plan do ION's strategists start to put into place?

This is a problem faced by most global suppliers today, as more and more of their global customers seek to reduce the complexity of decentralized, multi-supplier contract.

Fortunately, ION has all the pieces already in place. What ION must do is call a meeting of subsidiary principals and relevant headquarters personnel to deliver a strategy for global key account management, as many of its potential problems will stem from ethnocentric attitudes in the subsidiaries. The authors ran such a conference for a decentralized, country-based supplier of services, using a business game to test out the decisions which would be made by delegates in respect of a hypothetical global key account. The results were surprising to all and hammered home the need to subjugate local interests to the good of the global account. More importantly, it changed attitudes and paved the way for constructive teamwork across national organizations to support global customers.

ION has to address the following challenges:

● process excellence;
● cross-cultural management;
● thorough and effective communications, internally and externally;
● attention to detail over a huge scope of work;
● ensuring the whole team can see the whole picture (there may be hundreds of people devoted to a key account worldwide).

Case 11 – Étoile Consulting

Jeanne Étoile, general manager of Étoile Consulting, has just awarded the trophies in the annual Étoile and clients' doubles tennis tournament. She has been extremely proud to see the Étoile/customer doubles teams playing together – a mirror of the way her company works together with clients. It was particularly pleasing this year to see twenty-six nationalities represented in the tournament.

She spends her next day in the office thinking deeply. Étoile is recognized as the best practitioner of key account management in its sector. The company could be finished if it lost that accolade. How can Étoile keep up the momentum?

Étoile needs to keep abreast of developments in its industry and continuously to seek to provide solutions which provide superior value to its clients. Apart from this, however, Étoile could join a best practice key account management benchmarking club at one of the leading postgraduate business schools such as Cranfield. This way Étoile will always be at the leading edge of key account management best practice.

The company will also invest effort in the following activities:

- process integration;
- continuous communication with clients in-between projects;
- recruiting specialist skills;
- strong marketing communications and promotion.

Case 12 – Contract Employees Limited

Peter Piper has been the account manager for Discount Retail Limited for three years. Discount Retail Limited keeps all suppliers of goods and services at arm's length. All business is bid for on a one-off basis. Social invitations from suppliers are rebuffed. Account managers are very unlikely to meet a purchasing manager regularly, let alone a decision maker in another department.

Peter works for Contract Employees Limited. The company has been successful in regularly supplying temporary staff to Discount Retail's warehouse. Recently, a few vacancies were filled by another agency, who undercut Contract Employees' price. In fact, the warehouse manager was furious with purchasing because the staff supplied by the competitor were incompetent.

Peter is keen to persuade his managing director to take Discount Retail out of his portfolio and give the company to a junior account manager.

Then word gets back to Peter from one of the temps who had done an assignment at Discount Retail about the dispute between the warehouse manager and purchasing.

Should it change his mind?

This knowledge should probably not change Peter's mind. Discount Retail is clearly not the kind of key account with which a value-creating relationship can be built. It would be in the bottom right-hand box of the account portfolio matrix (see Figure 4.12 in Chapter 4). There isn't much potential for profit growth here and the relationship is poor. Accordingly, the relationship should remain transactional, with each transaction done on the basis of generating cash.

Peter may decide to stay just long enough to discover if the warehouse manager wins his argument with purchasing and gains higher level support for preferring Contract Employees Limited. This could establish a special status for CEL within the account which might enable the account to be reclassified in the account portfolio matrix. Peter could then move on to his next account having achieved some progress in difficult circumstances. The reclassification of the account would influence the choice of the skills required in the new account manager.

Case 13 – Components GmbH

Components GmbH has won a contract to supply newly developed sealants to a European manufacturing consortium, KFG. It is the only supplier of these parts to KFG. The entry costs were high, due to the unique customer requirements, but it is now unlikely that any competitor could follow. The sealants are performing very well, and Components GmbH has the opportunity to demonstrate more of its products. More importantly, the customer is very interested in the company's keenness to set problem-solving targets, to be jointly addressed and met.

Components GmbH has been given the opportunity to demonstrate its expertise in a very specialized aspect of its manufacturing process. An expensive, inefficient and dangerous cleaning method has to be changed. Components GmbH recommends an ultrasonic cleaning system, which fulfils all the customer's needs. KFG is now convinced that it is a business partner that it must work with.

How can both parties proceed, given that KFG insist that their requirements must be met through EU tendering procedures?

It is not clear why KFG need to advertise in the *European Journal*, but perhaps there is a public sector element in the consortium. If KFG are required to advertise contracts in the *European Journal*, then they must do it, and they must be very specific about their requirements. They can of course encourage Components GmbH to respond.

Components GmbH needs to proceed as follows:

- use its special expertise to influence the specification;
- use its existing knowledge of KFG to ensure it meets all the common requirements;
- provide extra, convincing information and analysis which should establish edge over any other tenders submitted.

Many selling companies with a partnership approach are averse to customers going out to tender. Nevertheless, they must remember that the customer will be required to market test their performance from time to time, and, if they truly are offering the best solution, an objective tendering process should recognize it.

This selection of mini-cases has presented just a small part of the myriad of problems that result from an organization's efforts to become more customer focused. We hope that you enjoyed thinking about these problems and are better prepared as a result for dealing with the challenges inherent in your key account relationships.

Bibliography

Academic books and reports

Bytheway, A. and Braganza, A. (1992), *Corporate information, EDI and logistics*, Cranfield University, UK.

Christopher, M.G., Payne, A.F.T. and Ballantyne, D.F. (1991), *Relationship Marketing: Bringing Quality, Customer Service and Marketing Together*, Butterworth-Heinemann, Oxford.

McDonald, M.H.B., *The Theory and Practice of Marketing Planning*, PhD Thesis, Cranfield University, UK.

McDonald, M.H.B., Millman, A.F. and Rogers, B. (1996), *Key Account Management – Learning from Supplier and Customer Perspectives*, Cranfield University, UK

Millman, A.F. (1993), The Emerging Concept of Relationship Marketing, *Ninth Annual Conference on Industrial Marketing and Purchasing*, Bath, UK, September.

Millman, A.F. (1994), Relational Aspects of Key Account Management, *Fourth Seminar of the European Research Network for Project Marketing and Systems Selling*, University of Pisa, Italy, April.

Millman, A.F. (1996), Global Key Account Management and Systems Selling, *International Business Review*, forthcoming.

Millman, A.F. and Wilson, K.J. (1994), From Key Account Selling to Key Account Management, *Tenth Annual Conference on Industrial Marketing and Purchasing*, University of Groningen, The Netherlands, September.

Millman, A.F. and Wilson, K.J. (1995), Developing Key Account Managers, *Eleventh Annual Conference on Industrial Marketing and Purchasing*, Manchester Business School, UK, September.

Payne, A.F.T. (ed.) (1995), *Advances in Relationship Marketing*, Kogan Page.

Ward, K. (1992), *Strategic Management Accounting*, Chapter 6 on Customer Account Profitability, Butterworth-Heinemann, Oxford.

Wilson, M. Marketing Improvements Group.

Yorke, D. (1986), The Application of Customer Portfolio Theory to Business Markets – A Review, *Third Annual Conference on Industrial Marketing and Purchasing*, Lyon, France.

Yorke, D.A. and Droussiotis, G. (1993), The Use of Customer Portfolio Theory – An Empirical Survey, *Ninth Annual Conference on Industrial Marketing and Purchasing*, Bath, UK, September.

Articles

Birchall, D. 'Managing the supply chain – a survey of executives', *Logistics*, February 1993.

Cannon, S. 'B is for benchmarking', *Supply Management*, 28 March 1996.

Cocks, P.,'Partnership in pursuit of lean supply', *Purchasing*, February 1996.

Cocks, P., 'Chains of partnership', *Supply Management*, 2 January 1997.

Hall, K. and Poots, T. 'Global warming', *Supply Management*, 4 July 1996.

Julius, D. 'Inflation: lower your sights', *Director*, May 1996.

Kennedy, G. and Webb, R. 'The game of strife', *Supply Management*, 25 April 1996.

Kennedy, G. and Webb, R. 'N is for Negotiation', *Supply Management*, 19 September 1996.

Lamming, R. 'Chain link offences', *Supply Management*, 14 March 1996.

Lynn, M. 'How partnership pays dividends', *The Sunday Times*, 12 May 1996.

Marsh, P. 'Gaining a harder edge from the soft option', *Financial Times*, 28 February 1996.

McWilliams, D. 'The state of the market', Chartered Institute of Marketing, Spring 1996.

Millman, T. 'Key account selling to key account management', *Journal of Marketing Practice*, Vol 1.1, 1995.

Nolan, A. 'Purchasing failure costs £2.4bn', *Supply Management*, 14 March 1996, reviewing *Profiting from Partnership*, A. K. Kearney/Manchester School of Management, 1996.

Partnership Sourcing Limited, 'Partnering for Success', CBI, 1995, reviewed in *Purchasing*, February 1996.

Ramsay, J. 'Partnership of unequals', *Supply Management*, 28 March 1996.

Stannack, P., 'Supply chain of fools?', *Purchasing*, December 1995.

Stevens, K., 'World-class perceptions', *Supply Management*, 30 January 1997.

Tyler, G. and Alexander, K. 'Building relationships', *Supply Management*, 28 March 1996.

Now that you have read this book!

It should be clear by now that key account management is a complex, multifaceted process that lies at the very heart of an organization's revenue and profit generation. It is far more complex than just selling and negotiating, involving, as it does, the skilful management of all the people and processes of the supplying organization, as well as exploring in depth the processes of the key account and producing a strategic plan to bring together two organizations in order to create value for both parties.

No organization does this perfectly, otherwise all key accounts would be at the synergistic stage.

Please therefore complete the questionnaire once more and compare your scores now with those in your earlier attempt. They will almost certainly be lower the second time around. This is quite normal and indicates that you have learned some valuable lessons from this book. It would be a wonderful bonus for the authors if you were to join your colleagues in making some significant improvements to your key account processes.

How advanced is your key account practice?

How well do you know your key accounts?

Score out of 10:

Do you:

Know your company's proportion of customer spend?   ☐

Know their financial health (ratios, etc.)?   ☐

Know their strategic plan?   ☐

Know their business process (logistics, purchasing, manufacturing, etc.)?   ☐

Know their key customers/segments/products?   ☐

Know which of your competitors they use, why and how they rate you?   ☐

Know what they value/need from their suppliers?   ☐

Allocate attributable (interface) costs to accounts/customer groups?   ☐

Know the real profitability of the top ten and bottom ten accounts/
customer groups?   ☐

Know how long it takes to make a profit on a major new customer?   ☐

Index